THE MAKING OF THE X FILES™

FIGHT THE FUTURE

CREATED BY CHRIS CARTER

BY JODY DUNCAN

HarperPrism

A Division of HarperCollins *Publishers*

HarperPrism

A Division of HarperCollins*Publishers*
10 East 53rd Street, New York, NY 10022-5299

We wish to acknowledge the following photographers for their contributions to this book: Merrick Morton, Michael Britt, Paul McCallum, and Angelo Vacco. Special thanks from Merrick Morton to Bob Wilde at Yashica/Contax and Teri Campbell at Meta Creations for their support and assistance during filming.

HarperPrism books may be purchased for educational, business, or sales promotional use. For information, please write: Special Markets Department, HarperCollins*Publishers*, 10 East 53rd Street, New York, NY 10022-5299.

ISBN: 0-06-107311-3

Printed and bound in Canada

Cover artwork courtesy of and © 1998 Twentieth Century Fox Film Corporation

First printing: July 1998

Interior design: Tanya Ross-Hughes, David Hughes/HOTFOOT Studio

Library of Congress Cataloging-in-Publication Data
is on file with the publisher.

Visit HarperPrism on the World Wide Web at
http://www.harperprism.com

98 99 00 01 02 /Q 10 9 8 7 6 5 4 3 2 1

INTRODUCTION

When I got the call from editor Caitlin Blasdell at HarperPrism, asking me to consider writing a book about the making of the *X-Files* movie, I had seen only one episode of the renowned television show—or, more accurately, the last twenty minutes of one episode.

Flipping through the seventy-two channels provided by my cable company on a Sunday evening a couple of months earlier, my attention had been caught by what I thought was an in-progress science fiction film. On the screen was a shape-changing being, pursued by a red-haired woman in a trench coat. Intrigued, I immediately stopped my channel surfing; but it was not until the "movie" ended and the closing credits rolled that I realized I had stumbled on to an episode of *The X-Files*.

I had heard of the show, of course, and write-ups about it had aroused my curiosity. As a devoted reader of mysteries and thrillers, as well as nonfiction books on the subject of criminal psychology, the show's suspense and FBI angles had appealed to me. I was also a fan of political intrigue, and conspiracy-laced films such as *Three Days of the Condor* and *The Parallax View* ranked among my favorites. *The X-Files*'s science fiction leanings also held interest for me, professionally. Due to my position as the editor of *Cinefex*—a magazine covering visual and special effects in the movies—I had seen and covered nearly every science fiction television show and movie made in the past ten years. Unquestionably, *The X-Files* was right up my entertainment alley.

But, except for this one accidental and partial viewing, I had never seen the show. The reason was simple. As the mother of a ten-year-old daughter who, from birth, had exhibited an alarming fascination for television, I had long ago instigated a "television-on-two-evenings-a-week-only" rule for us both. My big mistake was in letting *her* pick the two evenings: Tuesdays and Thursdays. Thus, I hadn't watched a show regularly on Friday nights, when *The X-Files* originally aired, or on Sunday nights, where it was later rescheduled, in years.

Considering my ignorance of the show, I was relieved that Ms. Blasdell, in that initial call, never asked if I was a fan. And I was even more relieved when tapes of the episodes began to arrive from Twentieth Century Fox, along with official *X-Files* guidebooks sent by HarperPrism. My first meeting with Mary Astadourian—series creator Chris Carter's executive assistant and the person who would be overseeing the "making of" book project—was less than a week away. Armed with the tapes, guidebooks, and magazine articles I had gathered on my own, I dove into the world of *The X-Files*, certain that I could become, if not an expert, at least a well-educated, familiarized viewer in time for the meeting. Five days of immersing myself in *The X-Files*, and I'd have a firm handle on it. No problem.

Only someone so unfamiliar with the show could have made such an arrogant, preposterous assumption. (I can hear the appropriately condescending laughter of thousands of X-Philes even as I write this.) The show was like narrative quicksand: the more aggressively I dug into it, the faster and deeper I sank into noncomprehension.

First, it absolutely defied neat categorization. *The X-Files* was often horrifying, but it was not simply a horror show. It dealt with aliens and paranormal occurrences, but it was not strictly science fiction. It featured elements of government conspiracy, but it was not just a political thriller. It presented two FBI agents as its main characters, but it certainly was not a typical crime drama.

Secondly, I soon realized that *The X-Files* was an extraordinarily complex, textured, and multilayered drama. What Chris Carter and his team had been creating for four years wasn't just a broad-brush representation of a world, populated by equally broad-stroke characters. These people had histories and families and fears and past liaisons and future dreams and complex motivations. They weren't easily defined as "good guys" or "bad guys," but, rather, were endowed with all of the ambivalent characteristics of real human beings. *The X-Files*'s heroes occasionally revealed weakness and fear, while its villains sometimes demonstrated strength and compassion. The world in which those complex characters interacted was just as three-dimensional. With each investigation or agency reprimand, one could sense the entire infrastructure of the FBI at work behind the scenes. Each mythology show seemed to be weighted with a real conspiracy that was as deeply entrenched as it was far-reaching.

So there I was, watching episodes in no particular order (since, stupidly, I hadn't yet figured out the numbered code that designated the chronological order of the tapes), reading through hundreds of pages of text, and growing increasingly apprehensive as the date of my meeting approached. I didn't have a handle on this show at all. All I had were questions. Who is this Cigarette-Smoking Man, and why does he have such a weird name? What is an "X-File," anyway? Whose side is Skinner on? Is Mulder nuts? And if he isn't nuts, why is he so paranoid? Is Scully buying any of this? How far up the governmental ladder does this conspiracy go? Who are the conspirators? What does Samantha's abduction twenty-some years ago have to do with anything? What is Mulder's father's connection to all of this? How could these characters have functioned before the invention of the cell phone?

With the possible exception of this last, all of these questions, I soon learned, were not unanswered simply because I was playing catch-up on a show that had been on the air for four years. These questions still puzzled devoted fans who had never missed a single episode—and that, I realized, was the key to the huge popularity of *The X-Files*. Rather than lay everything out for the viewer, rather than neatly tie up all the loose ends, rather than spoon-feed the television audience a simplistic narrative, the creators of *The X-Files* had dared to produce a show that, week in and week out, remained just a little beyond the viewer's grasp. Fans of *The X-Files* may have wanted to believe, but they *had* to think.

My mind teeming with images of mutants and spaceships and aliens and ghosts, I arrived at my meeting with Mary at least clear on which agent was Mulder and which was Scully—a distinction I could not have made with any confidence only a week earlier. And when she asked me if I was familiar with the show, I could answer, truthfully, that I was.

Fortunately, she didn't press further and ask me to define "familiar."

My research into the *X-Files* series continued as I covered the making of the feature film; and although, even now, I could be whipped easily in a trivia face-off with a real *X-Files* buff, I watched enough and read enough and listened enough to become fairly knowledgeable on the subject of this unique, intelligent, award-winning television show. And, in retrospect, I can see that my initial ignorance actually worked to my advantage in chronicling the film's production, for I came to the assignment without preconceived notions, without knowledge of the myths surrounding the series and its characters, without prejudice regarding how the feature film did or did not do justice to its small-screen counterpart. I came to it a relatively blank slate—as will many of the audience members entering the world of *The X-Files* for the first time through the feature film.

I am grateful that this book project came along, not only because *The X-Files* promises to be a major film event, not only because it provided me with the opportunity to work with writers, directors, producers, technicians, and artists of taste and integrity, but also because it was the catalyst for my introduction to *The X-Files*, one of the finest hours of drama on television.

I never miss it now. And television nights at my house have been changed to Thursdays and Sundays.

I: THE LEAD-UP

The X-Files was halfway through its second season when the Museum of Television and Radio in Los Angeles invited the show's team of producers, writers, and directors to headline a panel discussion and question-and-answer forum. They packed 'em in.

That had not always been the case. When the Fox Network series premiered in Fall 1993, it generated neither widespread excitement nor big ratings. A small audience did find the show, and was fiercely devoted to it; but its paranormal subject matter, paranoid undertones and dark, quirky humor did not, at first, resonate with a mainstream audience.

With roots that could be traced to the *Night Stalker* television series of the 1970s, *The X-Files* brought bold realism and a hip attitude to the "monster-of-the-week" genre through a simple, yet highly flexible premise: FBI agents Fox Mulder and Dana Scully investigate cases that defy rational explanation, cases dubbed "X-Files." Mulder is a true believer with a personal agenda: the search for a sister he believes was abducted by aliens as a child. Scully, a medical doctor who puts her faith in science, is teamed with Mulder to counter his flights of fancy with hard, cold fact, and to keep check on the rogue agent.

The show was created by Chris Carter, a Southern California native who had parlayed a love of surfing and a degree in journalism into a stint as the editor of *Surfing* magazine. But there was considerably more to Carter than a jock mentality and his straight-out-of-Central-Casting blond good looks. Carter had aspirations as a screenwriter. In 1985, at the urging of his future wife, screenwriter Dori Pierson, Carter submitted a screenplay to Walt Disney Pictures. A three-picture deal with the studio followed, and Carter spent the next several years writing family-oriented television movies. Though he proved to have a gift for the genre, his heart, as a writer, was elsewhere. "When you come to Hollywood," Carter remarked, "you're a beggar, and you have to take what they give you. I don't think I wrote anything for the first six or seven years of my career that was an original pitch of mine. I was writ-ing other people's ideas. But it was good schooling, and I really learned my craft in the process." Carter also wrote television pilots, and eventually served as producer on *Rags to Riches* and *A Brand New Life*—assignments that led to a television development deal with Twentieth Century Fox in 1992 and, subsequently, to his creation of *The X-Files*.

On the surface, a show that explored paranormal phenomenon and global conspiracies seemed an improbable stretch from lighthearted family comedies, and even more of a leap from the world of surfing. But, in fact, *The X-Files* was a natural extension of Carter's tastes and temperament. "My creating *The X-Files* doesn't make sense to people who don't know me," Carter observed. "But to people who do, it makes perfect sense. *The X-Files* came out of my fondness for movies like *All the President's Men*, which I've seen countless times. I thought that political thrillers had become a lost and forgotten and unloved genre; and so, I wanted to reinvent the genre a bit and bring it back to television. The show also came out of the kind of reading I do. I'm a rather intense person, and I like intense storytelling."

As creator and executive producer, Carter oversaw every aspect of the show, maintaining standards in the writing, directing, performances, and cinematography that were unusually high for television production—and that earned him, in some quarters, a reputation for being "difficult." "I've been labeled a control freak," Carter conceded, "but what I really am is a quality freak. If it's not good, I'm not happy." After a slow first-season start, that insistence on quality paid off in the second season, when the show began to earn a larger audience, as well as the respect of critics and the television industry, garnering seven Emmy nominations, including one for Outstanding Drama Series.

Suddenly, the show that had premiered so quietly two years earlier was the talk of the town, the country, and the Internet. Series stars David Duchovny and Gillian Anderson—the former, familiar to audiences primarily through his role as a transvestite on *Twin Peaks*, and the latter a virtual unknown—graced the covers of heavy-hitter magazines such as *Entertainment Weekly, People,* and *Rolling Stone*. X-Files magazines, trading cards, and a comic book series were launched. Bookstore shelves were stocked with *X-Files* novels and season guidebooks, both official and unauthorized. *X-Files* T-shirts, mugs, hats, posters, calendars, and even phone cards were available through mail-order. *X-Files* conventions were organized and well-attended. A popular *X-Files* web site was initiated, featuring publicity photos, online appearances by Chris Carter, episode summaries, and, most significantly, a forum where thousands of self-proclaimed "X-Philes" could post comments and engage in spirited debate about the show.

By the time the show's writers, directors, and producers appeared at the Museum of Television and Radio in early Spring 1995 during the second season, *The X-Files* was on a roll not enjoyed by a genre series since *Star Trek*. For the makers of *The X-Files*, the excitement in the standing-room-only crowd that night was a gratifying confirmation that their unique, dare-to-be-different show had made the leap from relative obscurity to center stage.

The night was significant in one other respect, as well. As an episode of the show ran on the museum's theatrical-sized screen, every staff member in attendance had the same thought: *The X-Files* worked on the big screen. "We could all see that it played beautifully," Chris Carter recalled, "and that the story translated to the theater environment. And that was when we started to consider doing a feature film. In fact, I think that night was the first time we ever spoke about it out loud."

The notion gained momentum as the show's weekly chronicling of disparate paranormal events evolved into a more serial style of story-telling. Increasingly, The X-Files offered interconnected stories that combined to create a sweeping, complex mythology involving an alien presence on Earth and a conspiracy by members of a shadowy syndicate to cover-up evidence of that presence. Through episodes such as the first-season cliffhanger, "The Erlenmeyer Flask," the second season's "Little Green Men," "Duane Barry," "Ascension," "One Breath," "Colony," and "End Game," and the three-part narrative of "Anasazi," "The Blessing Way," and "Paper Clip" that closed season two and opened season three, a bigger picture began to emerge—one that strained against the limitations of episodic television and seemed to cry out for a big-screen interpretation. "Those two- and three-part episodes were very successful," said Carter, "and, all of a sudden, it didn't look like we were just doing weekly forty-three-minute episodes. We were doing shows that were verging on feature length, stories that were worthy of a more grand-scale execution. And we kept hearing, 'This is better than most movies you see in the theater.'"

The show's underlying mythology continued to expand as The X-Files moved into its third and fourth seasons. During that period, the X-Files movie grew from an interesting prospect to a very real possibility—in part because, with his five-year contract with Fox nearly up, Carter knew that the fifth season of The X-Files could be, if not its last, its last with him at the helm. What better way for the first five years of the series to culminate than with a feature film? "We could have just done a big two-part episode at the end of the fifth season," Carter acknowledged, "as we'd done in the past. But we had the opportunity to take what had always been a big-screen story to the big screen—so why not do that? A movie would be a chance to explode the mythology wide open. It seemed a novel way to answer some of the questions raised in the show's first five years, while revitalizing the show as it proceeded into its later years."

While there was, as yet, no formal movie deal with the studio and no screenplay, Carter and his writing team went into the show's fourth season with an eye toward launching film production at season's end. Thus, a long-range narrative had to be constructed. Events that occurred in season four would lead to events in season five, which in turn would lead to a resolution of the story in the feature film. No one intended to make the show's next two seasons one long preamble to the film; but shaping an overall storyline that would lead logically to the movie was essential.

To some extent, Carter had known the arc of that storyline all along. "I've always had ideas concerning the abduction of Mulder's sister," Carter said, "and also about his family's involvement in the larger conspiracy. And I've foreshadowed those ideas in the series. The foundation has always been there; and because of that, no matter what choices we made along the way, no matter how the story seemed to redirect itself, we never veered wildly off-course. The overall story stayed on track."

With both Carter and executives at Twentieth Century Fox convinced that the summer following the show's fifth season was the ideal time to release an X-Files feature, plans for the film's production moved forward. A window of opportunity for making the movie fell roughly between May 5, 1997—when the show's fourth season television production schedule would wrap—and August 25, when Duchovny and Anderson would have to report back to Vancouver, where the show was filmed, to begin work on season five. (Normally the show would resume production around mid-July. The date was changed to accommodate the feature production schedule.)

Well before that tightly scheduled shoot could commence, however, a story had to be constructed and a screenplay written, tasks Carter was determined to accomplish himself. But, overseeing the television production schedules for both The X-Files and Millennium—a second series from his Ten Thirteen Productions—Carter was already burdened with a double workload, and time for developing a story and writing a screenplay for a feature film was virtually nonexistent. "That year was the worst for both Chris and me," said X-Files writer and co-executive producer Frank Spotnitz, with whom Carter intended to block out the movie's storyline. "Between The X-Files and Millennium, we produced forty-seven hours of television in that one year. We were in a permanent state of crisis, working very long, grueling hours. Yet, somehow, we had to find the time in the middle of all that to come up with a story for the X-Files movie."

Carter and Spotnitz managed to steal a few days during the Christmas break, devoting most of a much-needed vacation in Hawaii to brainstorming and developing an outline for the film. "We talked a lot about what the movie had to do," Spotnitz recalled. "We wanted it to be true to the TV show, for one thing. We didn't want The X-Files to become something else in the movie, just because we had a bigger budget to work with. Yet, we were also mindful that it had to be a culmination of something for the people who had been watching the show for five years, as well as an introduction of these characters and this story to people who hadn't." Using the same method through which they had worked out stories for the television series, Carter and Spotnitz sketched out scenes on 3x5 index cards; and, by the time the Christmas break was over, the entire narrative of the movie had been roughed out.

Upon his return from Hawaii, and with an outline in-hand, Carter looked for a window of opportunity when his demanding schedule might afford him the time to write the 124-page screenplay. He found one—but it was a very small window, indeed. "We were in crunch time," Carter explained, "right in the middle of the season for both shows. But I was able to block out a four-day weekend in February, the rest of that week, and the following weekend—which gave me ten days to write the script, or at least make a dent in it. I knew I would have to write ten pages a day, something I'd disciplined myself to do, since that was roughly my output on the television series. Fortunately, the story had been worked out with Frank over Christmas; and I already knew these characters well, because I'd been writing them for over three years."

To avoid the many distractions of his two TV shows, Carter returned to Hawaii, where he sequestered himself and began producing his self-imposed quota of ten pages a day. He was several days into the effort and making good headway when his computer started to malfunction. "One tiny drop of water got into my keyboard," Carter recalled, "and my computer went crazy. It wouldn't accept commands; in fact, it outright disobeyed me. It was a terrible feeling. I knew the sixty pages of material I had were safe, because I'd done backups every day. But I was still looking at having to complete the script either in longhand or on a rented computer—either of which would have been a drag, considering the volume of material I was trying to produce." Fortunately, an engineer at the hotel who knew something about computers was able to repair the errant machine within the day. Despite the computer glitch, by the time Carter returned to his office in Los Angeles, he had completed ninety pages of the script, just ten short of his original goal.

The screenplay Carter had written opens with a legend reading, "North Texas, 35000 BC." Two primitives trek through an icy landscape, in pursuit of something. The hunt leads them to the interior of an ice cave, where they are attacked by a tall alien creature with black, almond-shaped eyes. When the fight is over, the creature is dead; but his spilled blood—black as oil—pools and travels up one of the primitive's bodies as the action cuts to the same cave, present day, situated beneath the now arid landscape of suburban Dallas. A boy named Stevie falls through the long-sealed cave opening and is infected with the same black worm-like organism. The subsequent arrival of not only local fire department personnel, but a well-equipped hazardous materials team and a fleet of unmarked tanker trucks and vans suggests that this is no ordinary rescue scenario. Under the supervision of Dr. Ben Bronschweig—a research scientist working for the secret government project—a clandestine testing facility is set up at the site, and the deaths of Stevie and four firemen are covered up by bogus reports of a Hanta virus outbreak.

The project's tracks are further covered by an explosion of a building in Dallas where the remains of the boy and three of the firemen have been transported and secreted in an office of the Federal Emergency Management Agency. Agents Mulder and Scully—formerly of the FBI's now closed X-Files unit—are on routine assignment in the area, part of a legion of FBI personnel scouring a federal building in response to a bomb threat. Mulder uncovers the bomb in the vending room of the adjacent building; but when his superior officer—on orders from high command—fails to disengage the bomb, the explosion goes off as intended, and evidence of the alien virus is obliterated with the destruction of the four infected bodies.

One infected fireman is still alive, however; the alien embryo growing inside his withering, transparent body monitored by Bronschweig's team at the cave site. Within the cryogenically maintained host body, the alien reaches full term and bursts from the fireman's torso, killing Bronschweig. The dig site is quickly evacuated, the activities there hidden from future investigation with the hasty building of a community playground. Through Dr. Alvin Kurtzweil—a former colleague of Mulder's father in the State Department who currently makes his living as the writer of conspiracy theory literature—Mulder learns the real motives behind the destruction of the Dallas office building. Tracking down the remains of one of the infected firemen to a hospital morgue, Mulder convinces Scully to perform an unauthorized autopsy that confirms Kurtzweil's story of an imminent alien plague.

Further investigation leads Scully and Mulder to a cornfield dotted with bee domes, a site where the syndicate is experimenting with pollination techniques as a means of spreading the alien virus. When Scully is later stung by one of the bee carriers, her comatose body is whisked away on a plane bound for the Antarctic. Armed with coordinates and a vaccine given to him by the Well-Manicured Man, Mulder searches for Scully near an ice station, stumbling into the interior of a giant spaceship nestled beneath the ice. Inside, Mulder finds Scully within one of hundreds of cryopod life-support systems, used to control the gestation of the alien embryo. Breaking through the icy exterior of the cryopod, Mulder injects Scully with the vaccine and carries her to safety as aliens begin to hatch from the cryopods and the disrupted ship rises from the ice field and into the sky. With the disappearance of the alien ship and the burning of all evidence of the project, the alien colonization effort seems to have been subverted—until a final scene reveals bee domes sitting within a cornfield in a remote desert in Tunisia.

Carter's nearly completed screenplay was turned over to the Fox feature department, where it was enthusiastically received. Though still not officially greenlighted, the film was given a development budget by the studio and plans for production—scheduled to begin June 9 with a week of second-unit filming on a glacier north of Vancouver, followed by principal photography in Los Angeles—moved forward.

To get the production ball rolling, Carter immediately brought on producer Dan Sackheim, a television veteran who had produced and/or directed episodes of *Alfred Hitchcock Presents*, *Law and Order*, *ER*, and *NYPD Blue*, for which he won an Emmy. Sackheim had also produced the pilot for *The X-Files*, returning to direct several episodes during the show's first two seasons. Though the *X-Files* movie would be Sackheim's first feature film producing credit, that prior experience with *The X-Files* gave him a solid advantage in tackling the production duties for the film.

"Dan and I had always had a very good working relationship," Chris Carter commented, "and this movie was a chance for us to reconnect. I also wanted him for the movie because he knows production, in terms of nuts and bolts, much better than I do, and he has great taste as a director. But what I value in Dan most of all is that he puts the work above everything else. I wanted people who cared about the work, not about their egos or the power politics. I looked for those qualities in all the personalities that came on the movie."

Carter also knew those qualities to exist in director Rob Bowman, who had been on *The X-Files* as a full-time director/producer since the show's second season. Growing up in the film business, Bowman had embarked on a television directing career that included episodes of *Quantum Leap* and *Star Trek: The Next Generation* before landing his first feature, *Airborne*, in 1992. Attracted to the intense, well-written, and dark storylines of *The X-Files*, Bowman had returned to television to direct the first-season episode entitled "Genderbender," as well as the second season's "Sleepless." "At that point," Bowman recalled, "Chris asked me to stay on full time; and I've been there ever since."

Throughout their close association on the series, Carter and Bowman had discussed the possibility of doing a feature version of the show—discussions that took a more serious turn as *The X-Files* entered its fourth season. And in February 1997, Carter formerly offered the feature directing assignment to Bowman. "When Chris asked me to direct the movie," Bowman recalled, "I told him, 'Look, you don't have to offer this to me. I like the show. The show is better than any of the feature scripts I'm reading. I'm happy here. So don't give me this movie because you think I'll be unhappy on the show if you don't. Give me the movie only if you really want to give me the movie.' I guess he did, because he stood by the offer."

Although Carter had directed several episodes of *The X-Files*, particularly in its early seasons, he did not for a moment consider directing the movie himself. "Not only could I not have directed the movie as well as Rob Bowman," Carter admitted, "I didn't have the time to even *attempt* to direct the movie as well as Rob Bowman. Rob is a very collaborative person; and I thought that working with him collaboratively was a much wiser way to approach this than to try to do it myself. I could never have done my work in preparing for the next season of the show with the demands of directing a movie, which are incredible and

past anyone's imagination. With Rob and Dan, Frank and myself, we had four heads working on the process of making this movie. It was a very good, complementary unit."

Paramount in the minds of all four men was the issue of how to make the movie bigger, better, and more satisfying than what audiences were already enjoying on television every Sunday night at nine o'clock. "If people were going to leave their houses and pay good money to see a theatrical release," Bowman commented, "we had to give them something more than what they'd get if they stayed home and sat on their couches and watched the TV show. And the big burden that we shouldered was that the show had expanded to a point where we were already doing some pretty impressive stuff week in and week out—real spectacles with great stories and great performances. So, jeez, how were we going to top that? We knew that the expectations for this movie were going to be huge, and we wanted to deliver."

Armed only with that determination to deliver, the studio's tentative go-ahead, and a still-unfinished script, Carter, Sackheim, Bowman, and Spotnitz went into preproduction on *The X-Files* at the beginning of April, just ten weeks before the intended start of principal photography on June 16, and only nine weeks before a second-unit crew would begin filming north of Vancouver. Ten weeks was an excruciatingly short period of time in which to prepare so ambitious a film. Large-scale effects movies—which this one promised to be—typically would prep for eight months to a year; and six months was standard even for straightforward feature-length comedies and dramas. Yet, cameras

below: In the film's finale, the spaceship emerges from beneath the ice and takes off into the sky, partially obliterated by a turbulent weather pattern. The design of the ship started with Tim Flattery's concept illustrations, but evolved considerably in the following months with input from Chris Carter, Rob Bowman, and visual effects supervisor Mat Beck.

would roll on the complex *X-Files* movie in only ten weeks—and nothing had been done to prepare for it. No department heads had been hired. No locations had been scouted. No storyboards had been drawn. No sets had been designed, let alone constructed. A definitive shooting schedule had not been determined. A budget had not been worked out and agreed upon. Even the script in hand was a first draft that would be revised by Carter many times throughout the following weeks and months.

So much had to be done in so short a time, in fact, that just days into the preproduction process, Dan Sackheim approached Chris Carter about the possibility of postponing the movie until the following summer. "We were so under-the-gun," Sackheim explained, "that it just didn't seem as if we could get all of these elements together in time. Things were falling through the cracks because of the rush. By waiting until the following summer, we could have done our prep in the months before the series wrapped, and started filming as soon as Gillian and David came off the series, which would have given us more shooting days with them. We also could have had a longer production schedule overall." Despite the many advantages of waiting until the following

above: Chris Carter on location in California City.

year to make the movie, Carter and the studio determined that the time for the *X-Files* movie was now. "A certain amount of money had been spent on development, and the writers for the show were well into writing scripts for the fifth season—stories that were going to set up the plot of the movie. Too much of the machinery was in motion for making the movie that summer. To reverse that momentum would have been very complicated. The boat had already sailed."

II: THE PREP

Preproduction on the *X-Files* movie was initiated the first week in April, at production offices located just yards from the Ten Thirteen Productions bungalow on the Twentieth Century Fox lot. To protect its secrecy, the project was given a code title: "Blackwood." In the following weeks, the "code" was broken by resourceful X-Philes, and the Internet was abuzz with speculation as to the meaning of the title. Some suggested that it had links to a story by Edgar Allan Poe. Others insisted that it referred to Fox Mulder's interest in a MTV VJ named

Nina Blackwood. "Unfortunately," Frank Spotnitz commented, "the truth isn't nearly as interesting. Chris wanted some kind of code name, and he'd come up with something like 'The Black Project.' But I said, 'You can't call it that—that sounds *exactly* like something from *The X-Files*.' So we threw around other ideas, 'black this' and 'black that.' Finally, we came up with 'Blackwood.' We liked that because it didn't have an *X-Files* ring to it at all."

For the first couple of weeks of preproduction, as Carter completed his television production schedule and Bowman attended to storyboarding duties, Dan Sackheim was alone in the production office, interviewing and hiring key personnel for the film. First on his agenda was the hiring of an executive producer who would tend to the logistical and budgetary concerns of the production.

A qualified, experienced executive producer was found in the person of Lata Ryan, who had been an associate producer on Steven Spielberg's *Jurassic Park* and had gone on to produce *Fluke, Grosse Pointe Blank,* and *Tempting Fate.* Sackheim had become aware of Ryan through producer and director Frank Marshall, and she was soon brought in for an interview. Afterward, Ryan sat in Sackheim's office to read the script, since—in an atmosphere of paranoia that would make Mulder look like a trusting soul—no one was allowed to leave the premises with the top-secret screenplay. Secrecy was so crucial, all of the prospective department heads brought in for interviews were required to read the script under the watchful eye of the Ten Thirteen Productions staff. Many members of the crew would never read the script at all; and the few copies that were handed out were printed on red paper that could not be photocopied. "We had a unique situation," Chris Carter explained, "in that we had an upcoming television season that was going to lead up to the movie. If the secrecy of the movie was spoiled, then that entire season would be spoiled as well. The season and the movie were structured as a serial tale, so I had to preserve the element of surprise if I was going to have these upcoming twenty-one episodes lead up to the big event of the movie."

Lata Ryan's commitment to the film was soon followed by the hiring of production designer Chris Nowak, director of photography Ward Russell, construction coordinator Bill Iiams, and other key personnel. "By six weeks before principal photography," recalled Ryan, "we had our whole team together—the production designer, cinematographer, construction coordinator, costume designer, prop master, set decorator, transportation captain. All we did for the first two weeks solid was assemble this crew."

Chris Nowak—a trained architect who had worked as a professional theater set designer for eight years before entering the film business as an art director—came on to the *X-Files* movie through Dan Sackheim, with whom he had worked previously on a television production. Sackheim's positive experience with Nowak led to his being called in for an interview, even though he'd never served as the production designer on a movie of this scale. "In interviewing production designers," said Sackheim, "we tried to get a take on how they saw the movie. Chris Nowak had the best, most clear and focused vision of what this movie should look like. Rob Bowman responded to that vision immediately, and so we hired Chris."

Nowak started the design process by talking through the story with the filmmakers, formulating a sense of the atmosphere they wanted to create, both for the audience and for the characters in the story. "We really came at the production design from a story point of view," Nowak explained. "We tried to develop these places emotionally by asking, 'What do we want the characters to feel in this place? What do we want the audience to feel?' Dealing in those terms, we'd decide that one environment should feel dark, scary, and oppressive to Mulder, for

THURSDAY, JULY 10: LOS ANGELES

The X-Files is in its fourth week of principal photography. The crew has gathered at the Mira Monte Apartments in downtown Los Angeles tonight to film a scene within Dr. Kurtzweil's apartment. In the scene, Mulder—looking for answers from the conspiracy author—encounters Washington, D.C. police, investigating a bogus child pornography charge meant to discredit the doctor, played by Martin Landau.

The area surrounding the apartment building looks like a war command post. Trailers, equipment trucks, electrical generators, and production vans surround the building and spill over onto the blacktop of a high school across the street, where crew members not on active duty kill time with a spirited game of basketball.

Residents of the apartment building go on with their evening routines, seemingly unaffected by the more than one hundred film crew members who bustle through the halls and outer courtyards, carrying light, camera, and sound equipment. They have suffered such Hollywood-style invasions before, as the specific apartment serving as Kurtzweil's Washington, D.C. home is regularly rented out to film companies. "This apartment is booked solid for the next three weeks," producer Lata Ryan remarks. "We prepped it for three days; we're shooting it tonight, and then it will take two days to strike it. And there is another film company coming in on Saturday. It is always being used, and the occupant just lives in a small part of it. Five thousand dollars a day is a typical location shoot fee, so it's a good way to pay the rent. There are a lot of places like this in town that all the location managers know about."

The small apartment itself is filled to capacity with set pieces, camera and sound equipment, crew members, and a cast that includes David Duchovny, Larry Joshua as a police detective, and several uniformed extras portraying police officers. First assistant director Josh McLaglen calls out, "Background, step in please," and the extras take their places around the apartment, squeezing past crew members and gingerly stepping over cables and wires stretched out on the floor.

It is nearly nine o'clock at night when Ryan, McLaglen, and Dan Sackheim huddle for an impromptu meeting with Rob Bowman. The interior shoot is taking longer than expected, and everyone is concerned that the sun will be rising by the time the company moves to its second location of the night, the Chalfonte Apartments, a few blocks away. There, the second half of the night's shoot is supposed to be dedicated to exteriors of Mulder entering and exiting Kurtzweil's apartment building, as well as a scene between Mulder and Kurtzweil as the latter hides from the police.

The meeting is tense, but a consensus is reached: the interior shoot here must wrap in the next couple of hours to ensure that the shots scheduled for the second location can be completed before sunrise tomorrow morning. Bowman agrees with the assessment of the situation; but the time constraint is a blow, and he sighs wearily as he walks back into the apartment to resume shooting. "Poor Rob," Lata Ryan murmurs as he walks away, "there's never enough time...."

example. We talked through the whole movie that way; and from those discussions, I got an idea of what they wanted." Though familiar with the production design style of the television show, Nowak chose not to review episodes as a means of preparing for the movie. "I wanted the movie to be as fresh and new as possible in its design. Of course, there were some elements from the show that had to be retained, just for continuity. The look of Scully's and Mulder's apartments, for instance, had already been established in the show, and were recreated for the movie, more or less exactly."

The overwhelming challenge for Nowak, as it would be for every department head, was the limited time period between his hiring and the onset of production. "We had only eight weeks in which to find all of the locations, conceive the sets—most of which were huge and complicated—draw up plans for the sets and start building them," Nowak stated. Guided by input from the filmmakers and his general knowledge of the show, Nowak began by generating artwork for the major sets and locations, working with concept artists Tim Flattery and Jim Martin. "I'd do very rough sketches first, just to make sure we were going in the right direction. Then I would give those roughs to Tim and Jim, who would develop them and finish them out. Tim was particularly good at rendering big landscapes in watercolor and wash and pencil paintings. Jim worked mostly in graphite, doing very tight, extremely detailed pictures, right down to sunglasses sitting on a table. Between those two illustrators, we got everything we needed in our concept illustrations." Fully developed artwork was presented to Carter, Sackheim, Bowman, and Ryan for approval. "Fortunately, considering the time schedule, they never made a lot of changes. All of our talking beforehand had aimed us in a single direction, right from the beginning. There continued to be a development of ideas, but those ideas were built on the foundation that had already been laid."

Once approved, set concepts went to the blueprint stage so that construction could begin, under the supervision of construction coordinator Bill Iiams. Rather than build sets consecutively and in an order determined by the shooting schedule—the standard set-building approach—the art department and construction crews were required to begin construction on all of the major sets for the *X-Files* movie simultaneously. "We *had* to start everything at once," Nowak commented, "because our time up front was so short. As soon as all the drawings and blueprints were done, we asked to have all of the stages we would be shooting on opened immediately, so that we could start building. Production didn't want to do that, because it meant they had to start paying rent on all of the stages right from the beginning. But it was the only way to get the job done in time. We had only seven weeks before some of these sets would be shot. And even the sets that wouldn't be shot until later in the schedule required a lot of pre-rigging. We had to get going right away and create some momentum."

Major stage sets included the interior of the spaceship, the exterior spaceship ice field, and a cave set that would serve as both the ice cave featured in the film's opening and the modern-day cave where Stevie falls and Dr. Bronschweig sets up his testing facility. In addition to stage sets, Nowak and his art department had to prepare various location settings. Art directors Marc Fisichella and Greg Bolton divided the art department responsibilities, with the former overseeing locations, and the latter orchestrating the stage sets.

Working in tandem with Nowak and the art department was director of photography Ward Russell, also hired near the beginning of the

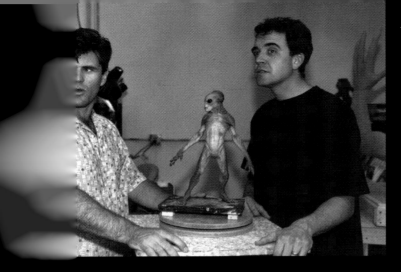

movie project to come along when *The X-Files* fell into my lap," R
said. "It was a last-minute thing. I had the meeting with the produ
on Friday, was hired that afternoon, and started work on the follo
Monday." Russell immediately began to study episodes of the sho
gain an understanding of *The X-Files*'s established photographic s
"Dan and Rob said in our first meeting that they wanted to expand
that body of work. They wanted to increase the production values
the scale of what already existed—not to duplicate what had bee
done on the show, but to use that as a starting point for forging ne
ground." In addition to studying the show, Russell conducted info
research, asking colleagues what came to their minds when they
thought of *The X-Files*'s visual style. "The two words that everybo
used were 'dark' and 'smoke,' and I used those words as my jump
off point. But after more discussion with Rob, I learned that smoke
been used a lot in the earlier seasons, and not as much in the late
sons, as they'd tried to go for a more realistic look. Rob explained
they had moved toward more sophisticated types of photography,
shades of black to gray to white, as opposed to obscuring everyth
with smoke or blaring lights. That was the direction they wanted t
in for the movie, as well, although, with this kind of movie, you ca
never totally get away from cinematic tricks. This was a science f
picture and a thriller, and that kind of film lends itself to some styl
tion." Russell also spent the few weeks prior to principal photogra
assembling his camera, lighting, and grip crews—consisting of a
mately eight people each—as well as the ten to thirty crew memb
required for rigging and striking the lighting setups.

While the production design and cinematography crews geare
for production, Tom Woodruff and Alec Gillis of Amalgamated Dyn
Incorporated began their early work on the film's creature effects.
had been a known quantity to the executives at Fox prior to their s
on to *The X-Files*, as the company had created the aliens for the s

production schedule. Russell had been shooting a commercial at
ustrial Light & Magic in San Rafael when he was asked to come to
Angeles the next day for an interview. To give Russell the chance to
iliarize himself with the story, Lata Ryan arranged for a production
istant to fly to San Francisco with a script. "Ward read the script in
room while the production assistant sat in the lobby downstairs,"
n recalled. "Then the PA turned around and flew back. It was crazy,
at least it gave Ward the opportunity to read the script so that he
ld have an intelligent conversation with us the next day. We were
y six weeks away from shooting at that point, and we really needed
P. Ward seemed to be the guy, and he got the job right away."
Russell's credits included *Days of Thunder* and *The Last Boy Scout*,
well as numerous commercials. "I'd been waiting for a really good

last two installments of the *Alien* saga. In fact, the ADI team was still on the Fox lot, finishing up its work on *Alien Resurrection* as the *X-Files* movie prepared to go into production. "Fox had liked our work on *Alien Resurrection*," Woodruff recalled. "They told us that the *X-Files* movie was going to be happening very quickly, and they asked if we would be interested in doing it. We thought it would be a great project, just because of the stature of the television show. So we said, 'Sure, we'd be interested.'"

When the producers saw the company's portfolio—which included not only the *Alien* films, but also *Jumanji* and several other high-profile, large-scale projects—they were as inclined as the studio to go with ADI

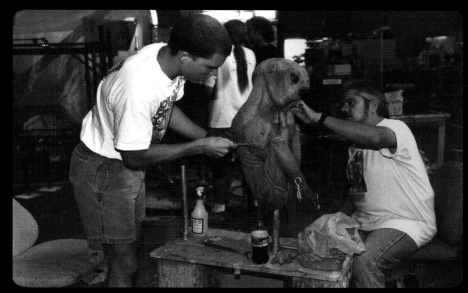

for the movie's creature effects. "We loved their work," said Lata Ryan, "so we went with them right away, without even bidding other companies. With such a short time before we started shooting, we didn't have the luxury of going through a lengthy bidding process anyway. We made a good-faith deal with ADI immediately, which allowed them to go ahead and start designing the creature."

Despite the fact that the producers had scheduled the majority of the creature work toward the latter part of the shooting schedule, the prep time was the shortest ADI had ever faced. "Most of the creature work didn't involve David or Gillian," explained Dan Sackheim, "so we were able to schedule it at the end of production, which would be after they'd left. That gave ADI the maximum amount of time to design and build the creatures, but it was still too little time."

Coming on to the project in April, Gillis finished out ADI's obligations to *Alien Resurrection,* while Woodruff left to start the creature design process with Carter, Sackheim, and Bowman. "The initial concept," Woodruff said, "was that the creature would be reminiscent of the classic gray alien—the little bald guy with the big, almond-shaped eyes and the little slits for nose and mouth—but that we could push it in a new direction. The idea was to come up with something that, if sighted, might lead someone to describe it as the typical gray alien. So even though we had some freedom and leeway in how we designed this thing, we had to keep the gray's basic features in mind."

Two versions of the creature had to be designed: a primitive alien that would be featured in the film's opening sequence, and a more evolved, modern-day version for the Bronschweig attack sequence and scenes within the spaceship interior. Due to the limited time available in which to build both creatures, however, Woodruff and Gillis designed the two so that their differences would be more cosmetic than structural. "There was so little time to get these creatures done," Woodruff commented, "we decided to build only one version from scratch, and make it look like two different creatures through the paint job and other finishing details. We did take the time to sculpt two different heads—a primitive head and a modern head—but the bodies were made from a single sculpture."

Ultimately, the modern alien was designed as a light-colored, smooth-skinned creature, while the primitive alien was darker in color, with a rougher, more textured skin and prominent hollowness in the cheeks and temples. "Our thinking," explained Alec Gillis, "was that the

opposite, top: Alec Gillis and Tom Woodruff, founders of makeup effects company ADI, present a maquette of the creature for approval. **opposite, bottom:** Storyboard artist Gabriel Hardman works as spaceship interior dummies look on. **above, top:** ADI artists at work on the alien embryo, which would be viewed within withered, transparent host bodies. **bottom:** Frank Spotnitz, Rob Bowman, Dan Sackheim, and Chris Carter on stage at Fox.

modern aliens were also newborns, since you see them in the movie shortly after they have burst from host bodies. As newborns, their skin would naturally be softer and less wrinkled. But the primitive alien has supposedly been around for a while by the time we see him fight the primitives. He has been living and hunting and killing in the harsh environment of the ice fields, so he would look more weathered and worn."

The design of both versions started with sketches drawn by ADI artists Jordu Schell, Andy Schoneberg, and David Perteet. Once those sketches had been refined and approved, Schell created a ten-inch-tall maquette that enabled the filmmakers to see the design in three dimensions. "We made a few minor changes from there," said Woodruff, "mainly in the eyes. It took a few passes to get the eyes just right, because everybody felt the eyes were so key to showing the character of this alien. The creature had to look benign and nonthreatening at

above: The ADI shop, populated by host dummies. **left:** An ADI crew member finalizes a sculpture, made of clear silicone to create a gelatinous, fleshy skin. **opposite, top:** Silicone bodies were set in fiberglass molds. **opposite, bottom:** An ADI makeup effects artist punches hair into the scalp of one of the host bodies.

certain times, yet fierce and frightening when it was attacking. Chris Carter was also specific about wanting the creature to look as if it had some wisdom in its features."

ADI worked feverishly to complete its designs as the few precious weeks of preproduction flew by. It was not until the final weeks of that preproduction phase that a visual effects supervisor was hired. Although the producers had opted against going through a bidding process for the assignment of the creature effects, three visual effects companies were invited to bid on the show—a luxury that was afford-able, time-wise, due to the fact that little preparatory work would be demanded of the visual effects team. The nature of visual effects was such that the team's efforts would be executed either on the set, during production, or in the postproduction phase, after filming had wrapped, when the visual effects shots would be generated.

Ultimately, the visual effects supervisor role was assigned to Mat Beck of Light Matters, who had served in that same capacity for the first three seasons of *The X-Files* before leaving in 1997 to supervise the effects for *Volcano*. "We were considering these bids," said Lata Ryan, "when Chris Carter said, 'You know, I was always real happy with Mat Beck on the show. Why don't we just go with him?' It was clear that Chris wanted Mat Beck, so as far as I was concerned, we were going to get Mat Beck."

"We encouraged Mat to bid," Dan Sackheim elaborated, "and we considered his bid, along with those from several large companies. In the end, we felt more comfortable going with Mat because we knew him, and we knew he would be on the same page, aesthetically, as we were. Also, we realized that we were going to be very hands-on and give a lot of input. Some of the bigger effects companies require a fair amount of autonomy in terms of design and execution, and that wouldn't have been a good fit for us. Mat had the ability to capture what we had in our minds; and our previous relationship with him allowed us to communicate with a bit of shorthand."

Although Beck was not under the gun during the prep period to the same degree as the other department heads, he did have to assemble his team and prepare for the filming of visual effects plates during principal photography. "Mat immediately started attending all of the meetings," said Ryan, "giving us his input from the visual effects standpoint."

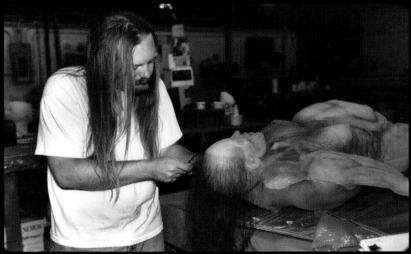

As preproduction activities continued in the art, camera, and creature effects departments, the producers turned their attention from hiring department heads to other preproduc-tion tasks such as casting—a process that would actually continue throughout production. The contractual commit-ments of David Duchovny and Gillian Anderson—vital to the feature film—had been sought well before the movie went into development, but negotiations with the stars continued clear up until the start of film-ing. Both actors harbored some initial doubts about doing the film, since it would mean spending their hiatuses playing the same charac-ter they had been portraying for the previous four years. "No actor wants to keep playing the same role over and over," noted David Duchovny. "So it wasn't as if I was jumping up and down for joy when I signed on. But I felt like it was the right time to do this movie. I liked the idea of doing it while the show was still going on, rather than after the show ended. I saw the logic in that."

"At first," Gillian Anderson concurred, "I thought I would prefer to dive into a different world from *The X-Files*. But as soon as things started picking up and it looked like the movie was definitely going to happen, I started to get excited about it. I knew it would be a good thing to be involved with."

While the movie's cast would include other series regulars such as Mitch Pileggi as FBI Assistant Director Walter Skinner, William B. Davis as the Cigarette-Smoking Man, John Neville as the Well-Manicured Man, and Bruce Harwood, Dean Haglund, and Tom Braidwood as the Lone Gunmen, the film would also feature such respected and well-known actors as Martin Landau as Dr. Alvin Kurtzweil, Armin Mueller-Stahl as Syndicate leader Conrad Strughold, Blythe Danner as FBI Assistant Director Jana Cassidy, Jeffrey DeMunn as Dr. Bronschweig, and Glenne Headly as a barmaid. The signing of these established stars broke with the tradition of the television show, which had typically featured strong actors that were, nonetheless, virtual unknowns. "I've never drawn on what I call 'marquee players' for the show," noted Carter, "even though many who are fans of the show have expressed interest. I've always resisted using very well-known actors because I think the show is only as scary as it is believable; and it is only as believable as it is real. As soon as you put in an actor whose face is very recognizable, you've got a situation that works against the reality of the show. But the movie was an opportunity to use those kinds of actors, people we wouldn't normally be able to put in the TV series; either because we couldn't afford them or because their faces were too famous. So when we got a chance to hire Martin Landau, we did it—and it was perfect casting. Casting Blythe Danner was a huge thrill for me. Glenne Headly is a fan of the show; so I asked her if she would be willing to do the role of the barmaid, even though it is small, and she said she'd be delighted to do it."

By four weeks into prep, production on the television series had wrapped, enabling Carter and other key players to focus their attention solely on the upcoming film shoot. Bowman had broken free from his responsibilities to the show even earlier, settling in Los Angeles and storyboarding the movie's major sequences with artists Gabriel Hardman and Rob Bihun—without benefit of having seen a single location or set concept. "None of those things had been decided yet," Bowman explained. "But I couldn't wait until all of the sets were designed and all of the locations were scouted to start storyboarding, because time was running out. So I jumped into it, winging it a bit at first." Throughout the next few weeks, Bowman, Hardman, and Bihun storyboarded and restoryboarded nearly every moment of the film. "It was an agonizing experience—very intense—because that was the process of really creating the movie. When it was done, I wound up with a storyboard book that was thicker than Webster's Unabridged Dictionary. That was the kind of prep I demanded of myself. That way, when I got on the set, I knew I would be completely prepared and ready to go. Before we ever started shooting, I had the movie I wanted to make on paper."

Occasionally, Bowman's storyboarding process was interrupted by one- and two-day trips, since the finding of locations was another major issue that had to be resolved during the short prep period. Initially, the filmmakers had intended to take the production to a number of locations, including Texas, Washington, D.C., Alaska, and London, in order to expand upon the scope and range of locales that had been available to the Vancouver-based television show. "One of the things they don't have in Vancouver is desert," said Lata Ryan, "so a lot of this movie was intentionally set in the flatlands of Texas, just so they could introduce a different type of geography. Overall, they wanted the movie to have a more international feeling to it than they could afford to do on the TV show. Using a variety and range of locations as backdrops for the film was a big part of the thinking."

Location scouting took the producers, Bowman, and production designer Chris Nowak on a tour of Texas that included Houston, Dallas, Midland, and El Paso, as well as rural areas in between. The Texas scout yielded excellent locations for the cave site and other settings; but, ultimately, the planned location shoot in Texas was dropped from the production schedule. "When we came back and started looking at the schedule and the complexity of this movie," explained Nowak, "we realized there was no way we could ever make the schedule if we started moving around the country to shoot." The slimming of the budget also compromised the feasibility of first-unit excursions to distant locations, and alternate settings were found near Los Angeles. Location shots that could not be captured in the Southern California area—such as exteriors of London—were relegated to a less expensive second-unit crew, rather than scheduled for first-unit filming.

Throughout preproduction, the filmmakers continued to hammer out both a budget and a production schedule. The latter allowed for only 72 days of principal photography—about ten days short of an ideally paced schedule. Making matters worse was the fact that, due to their commitments to the television show, David Duchovny and Gillian Anderson would be available for only the first 54 of those 72 days. To accommodate the stars' schedules, all of the scenes featuring Mulder and Scully would be filmed at the front of principal photography, with shots that did not feature the two actors pushed to the back end. Further, the producers determined that the only way Duchovny and Anderson could finish their scenes within the allotted span of time was by working six-day weeks from the beginning of the shoot until their departure. The overtime built into the schedule represented a huge, but necessary, expense. It also cost the filmmakers potential crew members, since some refused to commit to the grueling schedule.

Even when the schedule had been trimmed to its leanest and meanest, haggling with the studio over the movie's budget continued. In an atmosphere of tighter fiscal control, Fox was determined that the *X-Files* movie be made as economically as possible—a position Carter understood and respected, since he was also put off by the recent trend of escalating movie budgets. "Going in," said Carter, "I think there was hope on everyone's part that this could be a forty-million-dollar movie. But that just wasn't possible, considering the movie we wanted to make. We wanted to do things that were bigger than the television show, things that required more technical expertise, more time, and more money. There were also hurry-up costs. We had such a late start, all of the sets had to be built in a hurry. And whenever you build something fast, there are additional costs."

The budget would ultimately be set at just under $60 million, but the issue remained unresolved as the production start date neared. And even as a second-unit crew at the Pemberton Ice Cap, two hours north of Vancouver, prepared to begin shooting, as scheduled, on Monday, June 9, the *X-Files* movie still had not been granted an official greenlight by the studio. "We had to begin shooting on that date," explained Carter, "because, otherwise, we weren't going to make our schedule. We were working in a proscribed, definite window to get this movie done in time to get back to the TV series. So the start date was fixed. It couldn't be pushed back." With the crew waiting on the glacier, and the studio and the filmmakers at loggerheads, the *X-Files* movie was finally given its greenlight the day before the scheduled start of production. "It came literally ten minutes before the whole deal would have fallen apart. There were a number of legal, contractual impediments right up until the very end. And those impediments were not worked out, nor was there an agreed-upon budget until ten minutes prior to our drop-dead date."

III: THE SHOOT: ON LOCATION

The last-minute greenlight cleared the way for second-unit director E. J. Forester and his crew to begin filming wide, establishing shots of the two primitives trekking through ice fields for the movie's opening sequence, as well as shots of the ice station that, in the story, serves as a front for the subterranean alien spacecraft.

Before the arrival of the second unit, art director Marc Fisichella and a local Vancouver crew of six went to the glacier to set up the ice station set, which had been prebuilt in modular sections in Los Angeles. Due to the isolated nature of the location, crew members, film equipment, and set pieces had to be airlifted into the site by helicopter. It was a treacherous business, since thick cloud cover routinely prevented the helicopters from flying in or out of the area.

Visibility was suddenly reduced to zero one morning as the helicopters airlifted set pieces into the site, and the pilots had no choice but to drop their loads and turn around—leaving Fisichella and his crew stranded on the glacier. "We heard the engines of the helicopters fade away," Fisichella recalled, "and we knew we were stuck out there until the weather cleared." The helicopters had made their retreat at ten o'clock that morning, and conditions did not improve until six o'clock the following evening. "We were stuck for almost two full days, so we had to spend one night there, with nothing but our sleeping bags. Since the ice station set was a solid, practical structure, we kept building through the storm, and used the set as shelter that night. It was a good thing we'd done that, because we woke up to about six inches of fresh snow the next morning. And since the set had no floor, our sleeping bags were right in the snow. The cold wasn't too bad during the day; but at night, it dropped down to the low twenties."

Fortunately, the locals hired as set builders were also survival experts who were well acquainted with conditions on the ice cap. "I never felt I was in any danger," Fisichella admitted, "because the people I was with really knew what they were doing in terms of survival. They did try to scare me with stories of grizzly bears roaming the glacier at night, looking for food, which may or may not have been true. We didn't have any food for them to smell out anyway, except for a few health fruit bars. I'd like to say that it was a very grueling, hard experience—just for the sake of the producers—but, in truth, it was a great adventure. Not too many people get to spend the night on a glacier." The assembly of the set—which consisted of five fiberglass

domes, each twenty feet in diameter—was completed once the cloud cover had lifted and the remaining set pieces and other equipment had been located and airlifted into the area.

Filming of the primitives commenced with the subsequent arrival of the second-unit crew. To create the appearance of primitive men, actors Craig Davis and Carrick O'Quinn were fitted with prosthetic makeups designed and fabricated by ADI. The makeups were designed over casts of the actors' heads, taken many weeks earlier, since the primitive characters were first up on the shooting schedule. "At first," recalled Tom Woodruff, "they were looking at actors with big jaws and other big features—people they thought would be suited to playing primitive men. But we told them those types of faces were the *opposite* of what we needed, because when you put foam makeup pieces on a face with really prominent features, the makeup looks too big. We asked them to send us people with nicely proportioned heads and large bodies."

The final primitive makeups were made up of three pieces: a head and ear piece, a facial piece that included the brows, nose, cheeks, and upper lip, and a third piece consisting of the chin and lower lip. Contact lenses, hand-punched hair pieces, and veneers that created the look of yellowed, ground teeth completed the makeups. "The lenses increased the size of the cornea," explained Gillis, "and gave it that dark brown look, with yellow on the outside. We also made up wigs and eyebrow pieces, as well as sideburn appliances to create very sparse-looking facial hair." Although designed and built by ADI, the makeups were applied on location by makeup artist Lance Anderson and his crew, enabling Gillis and Woodruff to continue work on the creature and other effects at their shop in Los Angeles. Before arriving in Vancouver, Anderson and his team tested the makeup applications, fine-tuning individual pieces until they blended seamlessly on the actors' features.

Because of the rugged conditions on the glacier, the makeups were applied to the actors at the crew's hotel, prior to their helicopter transport to the filming site. More than once, weather conditions left the actors all made up, but with nowhere to go. "For four or five days in a row," Anderson recalled, "we applied the makeups to the actors, and then sat around all day, waiting for the weather to clear so that we could be flown into

the glacier to shoot. Finally, on the last day, the weather broke and they were actually able to shoot." Though only wide shots of the primitives would be filmed at the location—with all of the closer shots saved for first-unit filming on the ice cave set at Fox—Anderson and his crew applied the makeups in their entirety, just in case Forester moved his camera in tighter than originally planned.

The glacier also served as the setting for exterior shots of Mulder in search of his fallen partner near the ice station in Antarctica. Rob Bowman, Frank Spotnitz, and David Duchovny flew up to the site on Wednesday, June 11, and shot the establishing footage on Thursday.

"We were based in the town of Whistler," recalled Spotnitz, "and it was about a twenty-minute helicopter ride from there to the glacier. Once we were there, we had to be careful to walk along predetermined paths, because it was a very unstable area. Also, since you can burn very quickly up there, we had to wear maximum-strength sunblock, sunglasses, and layers of clothing to protect ourselves. I recall spending a lot of time looking for a place to shoot Mulder spotting the Cigarette-Smoking Man through his binoculars. We searched the whole area, and finally found a spot. Because it was elevated a bit, the wind was blowing really hard there. It felt as if it was going to knock us down."

Though he spent only one day of filming on the glacier, David Duchovny was deeply impressed by the location's unusual beauty and majesty. "I'd never been in a place that beautiful," Duchovny said. "It was amazing—so big and so lifeless. That location was really an announcement that we were doing a movie. Everything was big and outsized. I felt like Lawrence of Arabia out there." Some of the hours on that day of filming were devoted to shots of Mulder driving a massive, tank-like snowcat over the terrain. "I'd never done that before, and—not being a real motorhead—it is always a little daunting for me to drive those kinds of big rigs. I was showing off in front of the crew and all, but I felt the pressure. Actually, it was an easy rig to drive, but I have a fear of mechanical things, in general."

Duchovny, Bowman, and Spotnitz returned to Los Angeles on Friday and on the following Monday, June 16, the production launched into its seventy-two-day principal photography schedule. Despite the close, almost familial relationships that existed between Chris Carter, Bowman, Duchovny, and Gillian Anderson—all of whom had been working together for several years—the start of principal photography was, in many respects, like entering new, unexplored territory. The vast majority of the three-hundred-odd-crew members were strangers to one another. And

opposite, top to bottom: Filming began on a glacier two hours north of Vancouver, British Columbia. Members of the art department arrived a week prior to the second-unit film crew to erect a modular ice station set. In the story, Mulder would be seen driving a snowcat over the rugged terrain. Concept illustrator Jim Martin's rendering of the ice station. David Duchovny, William B. Davis, and co-producer Frank Spotnitz at the glacier location.

making a $60 million feature was a far different proposition than producing a 43-minute television show.

And so the first few days of filming were a period of breaking the ice, a time for Chris Carter and Rob Bowman, in particular, to ease into their collaboration on the set. Bowman had directed twenty-three episodes of *The X-Files* by the time the film went into production, and Carter had been intimately involved in each, as he was in every episode of the show. But as hands-on as Carter had always been, much of his interaction was conducted from the distance of his office in Los Angeles. Throughout the filming of the movie, Carter would be a constant on-set presence; and a methodology by which he and Bowman could work in concert in the hectic, seat-of-the-pants atmosphere of production had to be established early on.

The initial period of principal photography was also one in which the actors developed their big-screen working styles and rhythms. "It was a very different kind of pace," Duchovny commented. "On the show, we were used to running the hundred-yard dash, but on the movie we were running the fifteen hundred. We had to figure out how to pace ourselves so that we could finish. The hardest part was that we were spending entire days trying to get one or two moments on film. That's the way the process goes. And when you have that much time to get those moments, as an actor you tend to lose track of your initial instinct. It is very difficult to hold on to that when you're working at such a slow pace."

Bowman, too, had to find his footing in the feature realm, after working so many years as a television director. "For the first two weeks on the movie," said Gillian Anderson, "Rob worked a little differently than he had before. He would come up to me in the middle of shooting a scene and have talks with me about it—something he had never done on the show. But after those first couple of weeks, he went back to a more typical way of working, using the kind of shorthand language we had developed through the years. He could say every third word, and I'd fill in the rest and know exactly what he meant."

One of the adjustments Bowman had to make as he shifted from television to feature film direction was re-familiarizing himself with the wide anamorphic film format. When filming the *X-Files* episodes, Bowman had made a habit of taping off his monitor at the top and bottom to keep him thinking horizontally, as if shooting scenes for a movie; but the anamorphic format was even wider than that simulated by the taped-off screen. "In anamorphic," said Bowman, "if you want to see somebody from head to toe, you have to back the camera up across the street. But I thought this movie lent itself beautifully to the anamorphic format, and from day one, I was loving it. I tried to be conscious, with each and every shot, of using the entire expanse of that format."

below: FBI agent Dana Scully responds to a bomb threat at a federal building in Dallas. **opposite, top:** The crew prepares a shot from the rooftop of a building in downtown Los Angeles. **opposite, bottom:** Director Rob Bowman (center) discusses an upcoming rooftop shot with executive producer Lata Ryan, director of photography Ward Russell, and other key members of the crew.

"The eternal problem of television," added director of photography Ward Russell, "is that the TV screen is very small, so you end up shooting a lot of big head close-ups just to make the actors' faces fit on the screen. That approach works since, in television, you don't normally have the budget to build big sets anyway. But when you move into a feature film, you've got a sixty-by-thirty-foot screen to fill, so you've got a lot more set, more scenery, more environment. We still were going to be shooting close-ups, but we were using a film format that would allow us to extend the visuals, so that a lot more of the scenery would show up behind those big heads."

The first scenes scheduled for principal photography were those between Mulder, Scully, and Special Agent-in-Charge Darius Michaud (Terry O'Quinn) as they discover a bomb inside the vending room of the office building. The vending room scene initially had been slated to be filmed within an abandoned

above: Special Agent-in-Charge Darius Michaud (Terry O'Quinn) leads his FBI team on the bomb search. **opposite:** FBI Agents Fox Mulder (David Duchovny) and Dana Scully (Gillian Anderson) stay in contact with each other while aiding in the bomb search.

UNOCAL building in downtown Los Angeles, leased by the production for the first two weeks of principal photography. But while rooms within the building would be used for other interiors, the space originally designated as the vending room was judged unsuitable shortly before filming began. "It was an impractical space to light," explained Ward Russell, "especially since that set was going to need a lot of top lighting through the ceiling, like any interior, practical, fluorescent-light set. We would have needed six feet of space above the set to hang the kinds of directional lights I wanted to use; but the space just wasn't there."

City noises that would have interfered with production sound presented another problem at the site; and so the decision was made to shoot the vending room scenes on stage at Twentieth Century Fox. With the change in plans, the small vending room set was quickly erected in a corner of the massive Stage 15, one of the largest stages on the lot. "Shooting those scenes on stage actually worked out much better anyway," noted Lata Ryan, "because it allowed us to stay on the lot the first couple of days of shooting. It was a comfortable way to start out, knowing we were just going to the stage, rather than to a location in downtown Los Angeles. It gave us a chance to ease into the production schedule."

After two days on stage, the company moved to the UNOCAL building for ten days of filming both interiors and exteriors. Closed for the past eleven years, the building is maintained by UNOCAL at a cost of $1 million per year—still cheaper than what it would cost to demolish the structure—and is often used as a location by the film industry.

Daytime exteriors shot at the UNOCAL building included a rooftop meeting between Mulder and Scully—the characters' first appearance in the film—as an FBI team searches the adjacent federal building for a bomb. The dialogue-heavy, expository scene was a crucial one, not only because it introduced Mulder and Scully, but also because it would set up their relationship and some history of *The X-Files* for those moviegoers who were unfamiliar with the show.

Jumping into the key scene so early in the production schedule, and under the less-than-ideal conditions of location shooting, Gillian Anderson experienced some difficulty, initially, in finding her way through the scene. "It was a big scene in a big movie," Anderson explained, "so I was putting a lot of pressure on myself to make everything bigger and better. I was trying too hard, and I think I overdid it in the rooftop scene. It had a lot of dialogue, and there were complicated shots to deal with, and we were out in the hot sun on this roof. We worked nineteen hours on the rooftop scene in one day, and I never felt like I got my head and body wrapped around it." The conditions on the rooftop took a turn for the worse for Anderson when the sunscreen used by the makeup department to simulate sweat caused an allergic reaction on her fair skin, which broke out in hundreds of tiny red bumps. The actress was given a second shot at the rooftop scene when technical problems with the footage mandated a reshoot at a later date. "By then, I'd realized that a movie needs less in terms of performance than what you would do for television, because the screen is so big, it picks up everything. When we reshot it, we got the whole scene in something like an hour-and-a-half. That time, it just clicked."

Scheduled for the middle of the UNOCAL shoot was the explosion of the government building, a large-scale event that occurs early in the film. The one-take special effects gag required weeks of preparation and rigging beforehand by production designer Chris Nowak and special effects coordinator Paul Lombardi. The art department's contribution was to construct a false front on the sixteen-story building's first and second levels. That facade would be destroyed by the explosion, leaving the real structure intact. "It was a clever bit of business by the art department," commented Mat Beck, who was onhand to shoot live-action plates that would be combined with visual effects elements. "They essentially glassed-in a balcony of the building and an open area under the balcony, creating fake rooms that could be blown out." Loosely modeled on the explosion of the federal building in Oklahoma City, the shots were designed to look as if an initial blast was detonated low in the structure, followed by the collapse of the higher levels, as if the pins of the building had been knocked out.

Construction of the facade had proceeded as soon as the movie had received its greenlight, just three weeks before the explosion shoot. "We prefabricated as much of it as we could in our shop at the studio," Nowak explained, "then moved those pieces to the location." Made primarily of glass and aluminum, the prefabricated sections were attached to the UNOCAL building in the days prior to filming. "The facade matched the architecture of the building; so when you looked at it from the front, it didn't look as if anything had been done

Once the two-story facade had been attached, Paul Lombardi's crew moved in to rig the area with primer cord and propane for the explosion. Most of the crew's week-long work on the building, however, was focused more on safety precautions than actually creating the explosion. "We were doing this in downtown Los Angeles," noted Lombardi, "so there were the usual environmental and safety considerations. We had to get the appropriate permits. We also had to figure out how we were going to protect the rest of the building so that it wouldn't burn down when we blew up the facade in front. To protect the real building, we built fire walls made of sheet rock. Those fire walls helped to contain the explosion and direct it to a neutral area." Once erected on the set, the nonflammable walls were refinished by the art department to resemble the building's original Formica and aluminum surfaces. In total, approximately $50,000 was spent to protect the building from the explosives used during filming.

Final preparations for the blast began early in the morning on Saturday, June 21, but the actual explosion did not go off until six o'clock that evening. Day-long checks and rechecks of explosives, cameras, and lights were necessary to ensure the success of the one-take gag; and the preparation paid off when the explosion went off without a hitch. To ensure thorough coverage, eleven live-action cameras filmed both the explosion and simultaneous special effects gags such as cars jumping into the air as if hit by the concussive wave of the blast and desks being launched out of the building. "It took a good-sized crew four or five weeks to rig all of that stuff and make it happen at the same time the explosion went off," Lombardi remarked.

Not only did the explosion go off perfectly and as planned, the underlying walls of the UNOCAL building were left unmarked. "When we cleaned off all the protective surfaces,"

above, left: The camera moves in on David Duchovny as Agent Fox Mulder within the federal building interior. **above, right:** Scully, Mulder, and Special Agent-in-Charge Darius Michaud (Terry O'Quinn) inspect a bomb discovered within a vending machine in the federal building lobby. **opposite, top:** After discharging the agents, Michaud faces the soda machine where the bomb is hidden. **opposite, bottom:** Mulder evacuates the building with Scully. The action was captured with a Steadicam, a harnessed rig that allows for fluid handheld camera movement.

said Nowak, "there wasn't so much as a scorch mark on any of the building's real surfaces. The only damage at all was one window that broke as a result of the concussive wave. We had built a tunnel out the back of the building to release and direct the pressure of the explosion; but the concussive wave traveled farther than we had expected, and it broke one window on the other side of the building, which we replaced."

In addition to being captured by the fourteen live-action cameras, the explosion was filmed by three cameras set up by the visual effects crew. Plates filmed on location would be composited with model photography later to provide wider views of the explosion. "They couldn't blow up enough of the real building to make it look like the all-encompassing explosion they wanted," explained visual effects producer Kurt Williams. "So

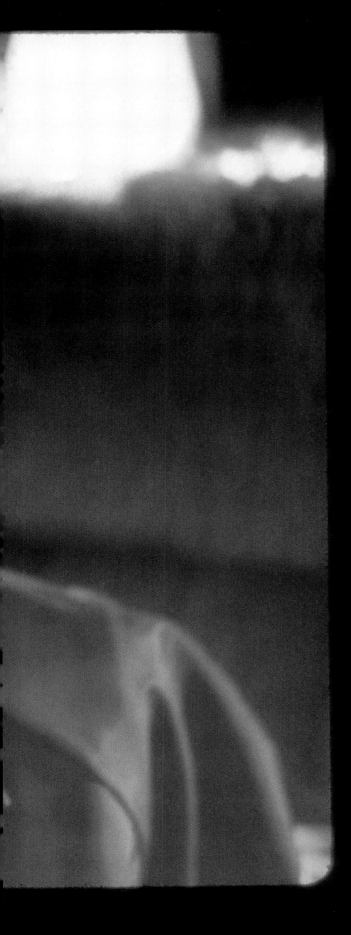

cally, knowing that the rest of the destruction could be done with miniatures."

To determine the proper placement of the cameras on location, the model shots that would be incorporated with the live-action photography had been previsualized through computer-generated animatics by Mat Beck's Light Matters visual effects company in the weeks leading up to the UNOCAL shoot. "Through those previsualizations," said Beck, "we designed three shots that we would create through a combination of the miniature and the live-action elements: a long-distance view of the entire building collapsing; a shot from the roof of the building, looking straight down; and a pan past Mulder standing in front of the ruined building." While the first two views would be made up primarily of model photography elements, the last would incorporate the model with live-action footage of David Duchovny in front of the real building on location. "The shot starts with Mulder and Scully getting out of their car. The camera follows them, and continues to pan as Mulder stops in front of the damaged building. In order to do that, on location we had the actors in the real environment, with a dolly camera panning with them. We put a green card in front of Mulder so that we could pull a matte and replace the fully intact building with the destroyed building miniature. All we needed was an area of green around him—about four feet wide and eight feet tall—so we could put that little piece of destroyed building in there. It was going to be a great visual effects shot because so much of it was real: the smoke, the actors, even sections of the building that would be split in with the miniature."

The following two days were spent filming additional special effects gags at the UNOCAL exterior, such as a shot of the car carrying Mulder and Scully lifting into the air as a result of the explosion, then swerving out of control and crashing. "Paul Lombardi really pulled that off," Rob Bowman noted. "We put a car on a flatbed trailer rigged with hydraulics to make it kick up in the air. We also had a propane explosion going off at the same time, behind the car. Through the limited view of the rear car window, that small propane explosion looked like part of the bigger building explosion. Then we fired a rubber material that looked like glass through small cannons, aiming it at a piece of clear plastic in front of the actors. It looked like it was flying up in their faces; but it was actually bouncing off this plastic, so it was perfectly safe. It all worked beautifully."

Interiors of the UNOCAL building served as locations for the Dallas FBI field office where Mulder and Scully look for evidence in the boxed debris of the destroyed government building, the federal building lobby, the morgue and pathology lab, and the Office of Professional Review room at FBI headquarters in Washington, D.C., all of which were filmed during the second week of principal photography. "We managed to get five different locations out of this one building," Lata Ryan commented, "which was a real convenient way to work." Like the building's exterior, the interior rooms required some construction and set dressing to transform them into the various settings.

Scenes involving the FBI review board and Assistant Director Jana Cassidy were filmed on June 25 and 26—a highlight of the production for the cast and crew, since the two days were spent working with the acclaimed actress, Blythe Danner. Also in attendance for the review board scenes was Charlie Parsons, a twenty-seven-year veteran of the FBI who had retired from the agency just months prior to receiving the invitation to act as the production's FBI consultant. The X-Files movie was Parsons's first film consulting assignment, a challenge he took on in the period between his retirement from the FBI and his new career as executive director of the D.A.R.E. drug prevention program in Los Angeles. "I'd never done it before," said Parsons, "but I thought it would be an interesting experience."

Parsons was on the set for a week, answering questions regarding the authenticity of the review board scenes and general FBI procedures. "These scenes were a critical part of the movie," Parsons observed. "Many times, you see things in movies, and if you are in law enforcement, or specifically the FBI, you know things would never happen that way. So I was there to tell them, 'No, it wouldn't happen that way.' Sometimes they were very minor things." Among the minor inaccuracies spotted by Parsons were briefcases sitting in front of members of the review board. "I told them that wouldn't happen. This was supposed to be taking place in the Hoover Building, with everyone coming from their offices to this meeting room, so they wouldn't bring their briefcases with them. It made it look as if everybody had arrived off the street instead of from inside the building. They also asked me if people would have nameplates in front of them, and I told them probably not. There isn't a board exactly like this one in the FBI, anyway." Parsons also corrected a line in the script that suggested Scully might be sent to the FBI field office in Des Moines as a disciplinary action. "I had to tell Chris Carter that we don't have a field office in Des Moines."

Before his week-long stint on the movie, Parsons had seen the X-Files television show only once, but he had experienced, firsthand, the show's widespread popularity and influence. "Every single time I spoke at Rotary clubs and such, I would be asked if the FBI really had an X-Files unit. The answer is no. There's no such thing. We have no paranormal group in the basement at Quantico or anyplace else."

One of the trickier shots in a later review board scene was a close-up of a bee traveling along the collar of Scully's jacket—a souvenir she has inadvertently brought back with her, after her discovery of the bee domes with Mulder earlier in the film. The production called in entomologist and film industry bee wrangler Dr. Norman Gary to orchestrate the unusual shot, the most complicated bee performance Gary had ever been asked to realize. "They wanted a single bee to emerge out from under Scully's right collar," Gary recalled, "walk a few steps, turn, walk across her back, turn again, then walk up and disappear under the left side of her collar. When I first considered the scene, I thought it was an impossible thing to do. For one thing, it was an interior, and it is much more difficult to control a honey bee's behavior indoors than it is outdoors, in its natural environment. Secondly, under all the bright lights used on the set, most bees would be inclined to fly, not walk. I honestly thought when I walked into this, that I was facing the greatest embarrassment of my life. I thought this shot just couldn't be done."

Gamely agreeing to give it a try anyway, Gary spent several sleepless nights figuring out how he might make a bee perform the specific set of behaviors—not just once, but numerous times. Once on the set, Gary used a pheromone attractant he had developed and employed often in his line of work to control the behavior of a single bee that had been carefully preselected for the task. "I chose bees that showed a tendency to walk rather than fly," said Gary, "then I took a few of those bees inside, under simulated set conditions, and selected the ones that showed a tendency to follow an aerial pheromone trail. We treated the fabric of Scully's coat with this pheromone, and I found that I could get a few bees to walk on that fabric, toward the odor. When we got on the set, I had a fan blowing the odor from the left collar to the right collar, where the bee I'd selected was released from a cage on cue. The bee came out of the cage, sensed the pheromone trail, turned toward it, and walked slowly across the back of the collar. Then, at the end of the collar, the bee turned upward and walked under the collar toward the source, just like it was supposed to do. That little bee repeated this same behavior about a dozen times that morning, flawlessly. Everybody on the set was astounded. And, frankly, I was just as astounded, because I

top to bottom: D.P. Ward Russell sets up a shot in downtown Los Angeles, which stood in for Dallas and other urban areas in the film. Mulder and Scully review the federal building explosion damage. On location, Rob Bowman goes over the storyboards for the day's filming. Paul Lombardi's special effects crew was responsible for rigging not only the explosion itself, but also attendant action such as cars being launched into the air via hydraulic lifts.

hadn't thought the bee would do it even once, let alone over and over again. That one bee was such a heroine, I saved her as a memento of this film after she died. To me, that bee was like Trigger to Roy Rogers."

Scheduled for the last day of the UNOCAL shoot, Saturday, June 28, was Scully's autopsy on the fireman's remains in the hospital morgue. In the scene, Scully determines that the dead fireman—burned in the building explosion—had been infected with a virus that had eaten away at his organs and blood supply, leaving him emaciated and pale to the point of near transparency. The morgue fireman was initially created by the makeup effects team at ADI, which was also charged with designing and building other transparent host bodies, such as the fireman under study in Bronschweig's cave laboratory and those discovered in the cryogenic life support systems within the alien spaceship.

"Except for the primitive makeups, the morgue fireman was our first thing up to shoot," said ADI's Tom Woodruff, "so we started on that first, taking a lifecast of the actor, doing a sculpture from that, then making molds and running our skin materials. But when we came to the set with this translucent body, Chris and Rob and Dan realized that what they really wanted was a *transparent* body. Chris, in particular, wanted a much more severe effect. He wanted the effects of the infestation to be clearer, even at this relatively early stage—as if once this alien virus is in your body, the first thing it does is suck the pigment out of you."

At the core of the problem with the morgue fireman—and with all the host bodies ADI would build for the show—was some initial confusion over terminology. "For us," said Alec Gillis, "the running joke of this show was: 'Is it opaque, translucent, or transparent?' Those terms are very clear to us, but not always clear to other people. We clarified the terms by telling them that transparent is like a glass of water, translucent is like a glass of skim milk, and opaque is like a glass of ink—you can't see through it at all. But there are many levels within each of those categories. A piece of skin could be transparent, but with some cloudiness in it that makes it almost translucent. It was very difficult to pin down exactly what they wanted these bodies to look like. Two-dimensional renderings meant nothing; and it wasn't something anyone could really describe in words. The only way to pin it down was to actually build something and show it to them, which was a slow way to do it. Even Chris Carter, who has a tremendous gift for detail and for understanding subtleties, had to see examples of materials in order to evaluate what he really wanted to see.

"The other problem was that no one outside the field of creature or makeup effects really understands these materials or all of the factors involved in getting something to look transparent. Transparency isn't just a matter of using a particular

above, left: Assistant Director Jana Cassidy (Blythe Danner) leads the FBI Office of Professional Review's investigation into the Dallas bombing. **above, right:** Agent Scully waits to be questioned by the review board. **opposite:** Assistant Director Walter Skinner (Mitch Pileggi), who is Agents Scully and Mulder's direct supervisor, is also in attendance at the review board meeeting.

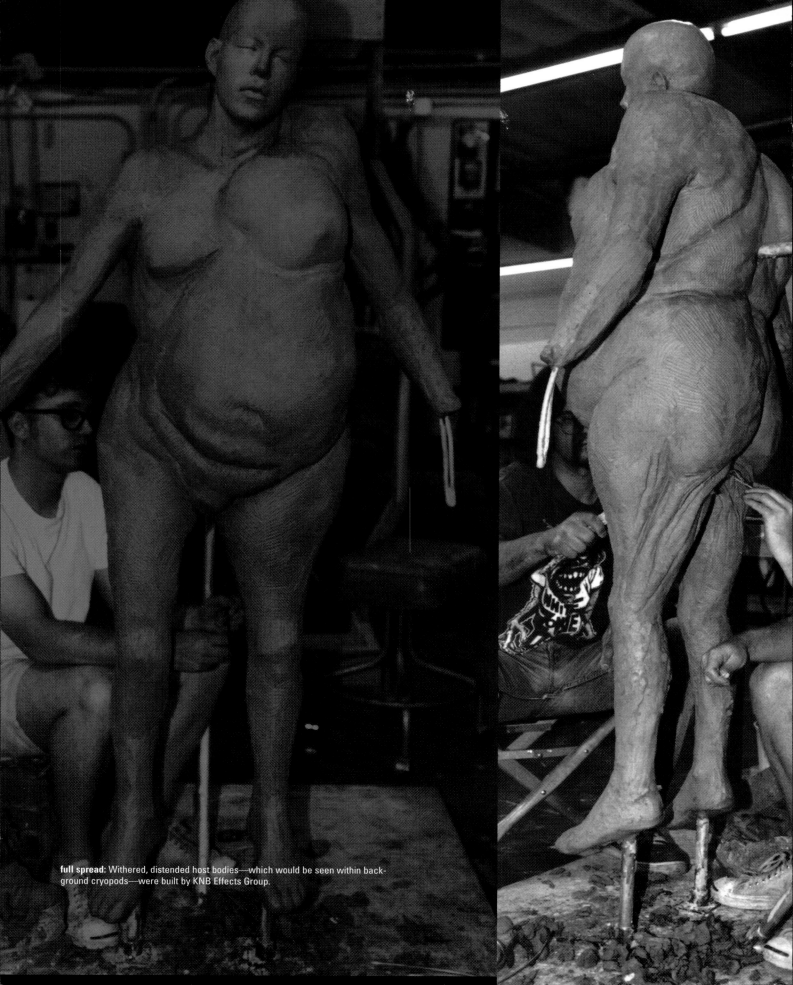

full spread: Withered, distended host bodies—which would be seen within background cryopods—were built by KNB Effects Group.

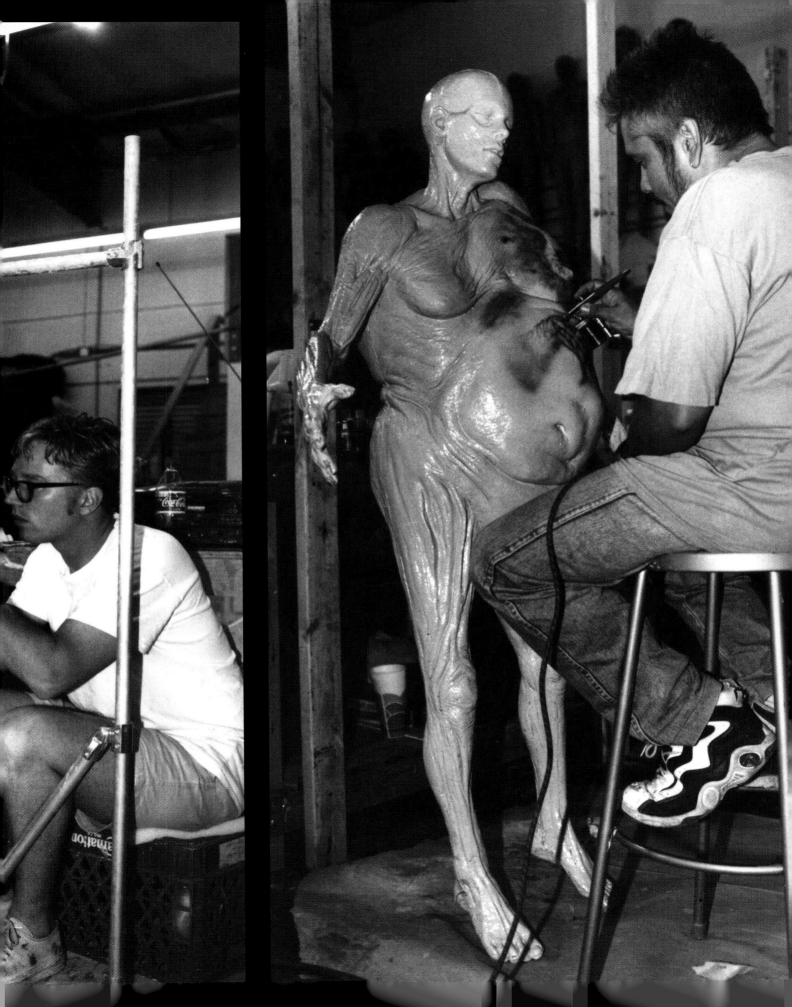

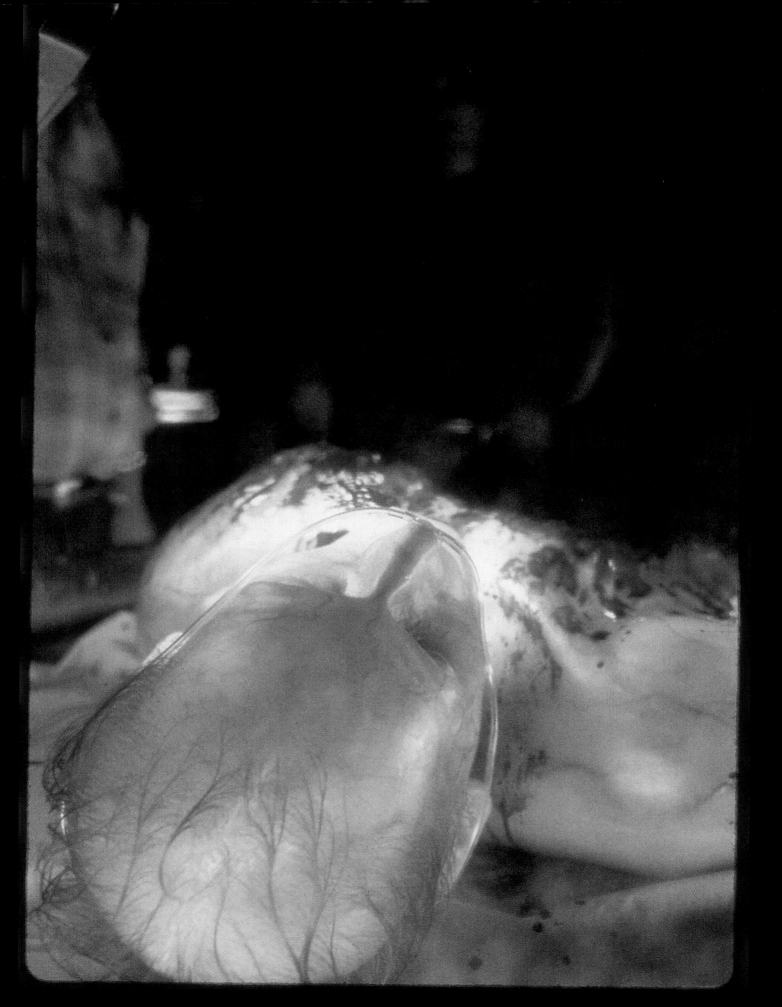

material; it is also a matter of form, the thickness of the skin, and the texture on the surface of the skin. It is very tricky."

The communication breakdown regarding the degree of transparency in the fireman body resulted in a final dummy that was unsuitable for filming; and Bowman was forced to shoot the morgue scene at the UNOCAL building without revealing the body itself. "The idea was to go back to the drawing board with the morgue fireman," said Chris Carter, "and shoot insert shots with the new, improved version later." Heavily involved in producing the aliens for the show at that point, ADI did not have the time or resources to go back to the drawing board and generate a whole new fireman, especially since the morgue scene was scheduled to be reshot in only two weeks. The first, rejected version had taken the thinly spread team six full weeks to produce. "We suggested that they give the job to a company that could concentrate all of its resources on getting this one thing done very quickly," Woodruff said.

That company was KNB Effects, which had done work for the television series and had already been brought on to the movie to provide support effects, such as host bodies that would go into background cryopods in the ship interior. ADI immediately turned over its fireman molds to KNB, where co-founder Howard Berger oversaw the sculpting of a new fireman body and the running of silicone skins for the final prop. A vacuform core on the inside of the clear silicone was sculpted to suggest fragments of skull and muscle tissue.

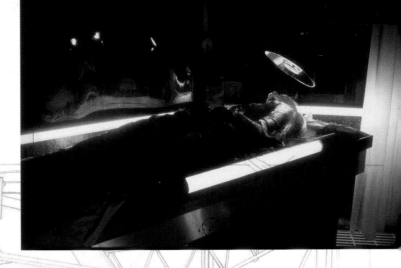

below: An ancient cave inhabited by a long dormant alien virus becomes a testing site, overseen by scientist Dr. Ben Bronschweig (Jeffrey DeMunn). **above and opposite:** There, an infected fireman is studied by Bronschweig and his team. The cave fireman was an articulated puppet built by ADI, and filmed within a massive cave set built on stage at Fox.

KNB and ADI worked in close cooperation throughout production, due to the overlapping nature of their respective effects assignments. ADI, for example, was building the "hero" host bodies—articulated versions that would be seen in close-up—while KNB was providing the background bodies. Clear and frequent communication was essential. Fortunately, the two shops were located within blocks of each other, and all of the principals had worked together before. "Alec and Tom and I know each other and respect each other," Howard Berger commented. "And there is a fun, healthy kind of competition between us."

Tim Flattery—who had been involved in the film from the beginning, rendering concept illustrations—was instrumental in coordinating the symbiotic efforts of the two makeup and creature effects units. "Tim was very important to that whole process," noted Carter. "He has very good taste, and he understood what we wanted. We were on the same page, so he was an important person to have in on the process of creating some of these things. He was our point man."

"Tim was very helpful," Alec Gillis agreed. "There were a lot of details that had to come together in a very short length of time, and Tim kept the communication going so that could happen. He would show our progress videotapes and KNB's progress videotapes to Chris, then get back to us with his feedback. He did a great job."

Despite the glitch with the morgue fireman, the ten days of filming at the UNOCAL building had gone remarkably well. Still, the inherent tensions of filming the populated downtown location and large-scale effects—especially so early in production—made the two-week period a trying one. "Everybody was a little nervous," David Duchovny recalled, "and there was a lot at stake, more at stake than what we're used to on the TV show. So people were doubting themselves, which can be really draining. There was a sense of 'do or die.' Everything had to be perfect. We were all aware that the work we were doing wasn't just going to come and go in a week, like it does on the TV show. This movie was going to be in theaters for a while, and then on video. It was going to be around a long time. That created a tendency for everyone to overthink themselves."

After a one-day weekend on Sunday, filming resumed on Monday, June 30, at St. Mary's Hospital in Long Beach. Working in the atmosphere of a real, functioning hospital, the crew filmed Mulder's escape, with the help of the Lone Gunmen, from a Washington, D.C. hospital—where he has been treated for a grazing gunshot wound to the head—as well as the scene in which Mulder and Scully con their way into the morgue to examine the fireman's remains.

The crew returned to downtown Los Angeles on Wednesday, July 2, to film a night scene between Mulder and Kurtzweil at Casey's Bar, an establishment bought out by the production for the night. The night also marked Glenne Headly's one-day stint on the show, playing the role of a barmaid who warms up to Mulder. Both interiors and exteriors of the bar had been shot by the end of the next night, when the company broke for a three-day Fourth of July weekend.

The alleyway behind the bar in which Mulder confronts Kurtzweil was filmed a few blocks from the Casey's location when production resumed on Monday, July 7. Additional alleyway exteriors—both scenes between Mulder and Kurtzweil and another scene in which Kurtzweil is cornered by the Well-Manicured Man—were shot over the next couple of nights. Some of those scenes had originally been written as daytime exteriors, but were changed to nights when location shooting in Washington, D.C. was ruled out. "Los Angeles looks nothing like Washington, D.C.," Ward Russell remarked, "so a lot of the scenes that were going to be day had to be changed to night to hide the city more. The challenge was to find

streets with trees and buildings that didn't look like a typical Los Angeles area. And the challenge from my standpoint was to light and accentuate those things that could pass for Washington, D.C. while hiding the things that couldn't."

The cramped spaces of the alleyway locations made both lighting and shooting more difficult. The longest dialogue scene between Mulder and Kurtzweil, in fact, took place entirely within an alleyway that was only four feet wide. To keep his camera moving, Bowman chose to shoot the scene with a Steadicam, a camera mounted to a parallelogram harness worn by a camera operator. The rig executes exceptionally fluid camera movements, while affording the freedom and flexibility of a handheld camera.

The Steadicam would be pressed into service many times throughout production in order to satisfy Bowman's preference for a constantly moving camera. "There is a lot of movement in this film," Ward Russell observed, "but it is very subtle movement. The moves are gentle, just to keep the audience a little bit off-kilter. Rob's style is not as static as some director's. He likes to move the camera with the actors. At times, that created something of a problem for me, because that much camera movement meant that the lighting had to be very flexible, and I had to light for a much broader area. With Rob, I never knew

below: The crew lines up a shot of David Duchovny in an alleyway location in Los Angeles. **opposite, top:** The Lone Gunmen (Dean Haglund, Bruce Harwood, and Tom Braidwood) play a pivotal role in the hospital scene pictured below. **opposite, bottom:** After being grazed in the head by a bullet, Mulder lands in a local hospital. The hospital scene—which also features Mitch Pileggi as Assistant Director Skinner—was filmed at St. Mary's Hospital in Long Beach during the production schedule, then reshot on stage in early March to clarify story points.

top: Despondent over the news of Scully's decision to resign from the FBI, Mulder escapes to a Washington, D.C. bar. The scene featured Glenne Headly—an ardent fan of *The X-Files*—in the role of a barmaid. **bottom:** The scene also served as Mulder's introduction to Dr. Alvin Kurtzweil, a conspiracy theorist who has important information regarding the secret government project.

where the camera was going to wind up moving in any given scene. So I had to light everything, just in case."

On Thursday, July 10, the company moved to the Mira Monte Apartments in downtown Los Angeles for the filming of an encounter between Mulder and Washington, D.C. police within Kurtzweil's apartment. As scheduled, the interior apartment scene had to be completed in the first half of the night, so that the crew could follow up at a location blocks away for establishing shots of Mulder arriving at the apartment building and a subsequent scene between the agent and Kurtzweil at the apartment exterior. "The biggest challenge of that night," recalled Russell, "was that we had a minimal amount of time to shoot this scene before we had to move to a completely different location for the exteriors. So we had to find a lighting scheme that could be done quickly enough to get us out of there in time. While we were shooting the interior scene, we had a rigging crew preparing the exterior site. But

even moving as fast as we could, the sun was coming up by the time we finished shooting the exteriors."

Friday night was devoted to another long alleyway scene, in which Kurtzweil tells Mulder about the plague that is about to be unleashed on the unsuspecting world. Because it was Martin Landau's last night on the movie, filming could not wrap until the scene was completed; and the long night of filming did not end until after eight o'clock in the morning on Saturday. "That alleyway scene was very ambitious," noted first assistant director Josh McLaglen. "It was four pages of dialogue between David Duchovny and Martin Landau, and it took a long time to get it. There was a lot of very technical dialogue in the scene, which made it that much more difficult." For maximum efficiency, given the structure of the scene, Duchovny had been covered first, with the camera finally turning on Landau at six o'clock that morning. "It was a rough situation for Martin Landau. It is tough for any actor to perform at that time of the morning, after shooting all night. But he was great."

"By that time," noted Lata Ryan, "we'd been working six-day weeks and very long hours for nearly a month. I was concerned that we were going to start seeing some real burn-out in the crew. But, surprisingly, morale was still very high. Everyone just rose to the challenge."

One of the greatest challenges of the shoot was still to come, however, as the production moved from downtown Los Angeles to the remote desert town of California City, ninety miles away. Cast and crew were transported to the location and billeted in nearby hotels on Sunday; and shooting there began on the morning of Monday, July 14. Chosen to stand in for rural Texas when the decision was made to restrict the location work nearer to Los Angeles, California City was the site of Stevie's fall into the cave, his playmates' run for help, the subsequent arrival of the Haz-Mat team and fire department personnel, and the scene where Mulder and Scully discover the playground. "Actually," said Chris Nowak, "California City didn't look that much different from the area in Texas we'd originally scouted anyway. It looked great, and it fulfilled everyone's wishes in terms of the desert look we were going for. In the end, I don't think anybody was disappointed that we wound up there, rather than in Texas."

The location—an expanse of desert adjacent to a housing development—had required some finessing by the art department to make it completely suitable for the production's purposes, however. To create the mouth of the cave, a fourteen-foot hole was dug into the hardened desert ground, then lined with a fiberglass plug. The hole was deep enough to allow the crew to film firemen and other rescue personnel entering the cave opening. Deeper interiors would be shot much later in the schedule, on a cave set built on stage at Fox.

Other than the fourteen-foot hole, which had been dug by a subcontractor the previous week, the area's natural desert landscape had served the needs of the production as it was. But when the contractor—uncertain what to do with the mounds of dirt he'd dug out of the ground—spread the new earth evenly throughout the desert field, emergency measures had to be taken to restore the location. "The contractor had scraped everything within a hundred-foot radius of the hole clean and covered it with a two-inch layer of this dirt, which completely changed the color of the ground," explained Nowak. "Instead of looking baked and desert-like, it suddenly looked like dark earth that had come from the hole. The color and look of the entire landscape was suddenly different. All the natural plant life had been covered over. The tumbleweeds were gone. It was a disaster." Greensman Dennis Butterworth and his crew spent the weekend prior to filming restoring the site to its previous condition, spreading lighter colored dirt from an adjacent field over the entire area, then artfully arranging new tumbleweeds and plants throughout the cleared

field. "Dennis and his crew did a beautiful job of fixing the location over that weekend."

A new member of the crew brought in specifically for the California City shoot was the snake wrangler. "Prior to going to California City," recalled Chris Carter, "we'd heard about the dreaded Mojave Green rattlesnake. Supposedly, they are quite poisonous and numerous in that area. To allay the fear of the crew, we hired this young guy to be our snake wrangler. He and his father specialize in handling and providing reptiles to movie companies. So he hung around the set during the days we were in California City, caught some snakes and put them in jars and showed them to the crew. It was a source of a lot of 'oohs' and 'ahhs,' but I don't think anyone ever saw a snake beyond the ones Chris had in the containers."

The California City shoot began with shots of fire trucks and other rescue units arriving at the scene, followed by the landings of the medevac and Haz-Mat helicopters, and the arrival of mysterious tanker trucks and a fleet of official-looking cars as Dr. Bronschweig takes charge of the site. Also shot in California City was a huge pullback from the cave opening. The camera, mounted on a crane, pulled up from the hole to capture a high view of Stevie's friends running to get help, then continued to pull up and back over the top of the neighborhood to reveal the Dallas skyline in the distance—imagery that would be composited into the shot by the visual effects team.

Of the three young actors playing Stevie's friends, only one had any previous acting experience. "The conditions at California City made for a pretty rough initiation for them into the world of making movies," Lata Ryan commented. "But all of them were great, especially considering that they were only thirteen, fourteen years old. Production paid for a pizza party for them and their parents on the way home from California City, just to say 'thank you' and to let them unwind from the stress of the shoot in the desert."

The crew's three days in California City culminated on Wednesday, July 16, with the filming of the scene in which Mulder and Scully arrive at the Texas dig site, only to find it covered by a spanking-new playground. The 140-by-100-foot expanse of green lawn, fencing, and playground equipment had been set up overnight by the art department. But when the film crew came to work that Wednesday morning, it was clear to everyone that the modest park would not suffice. "The park was much too small," said Rob Bowman. "It was a little dot of green in the middle of all this desert and dead bush and

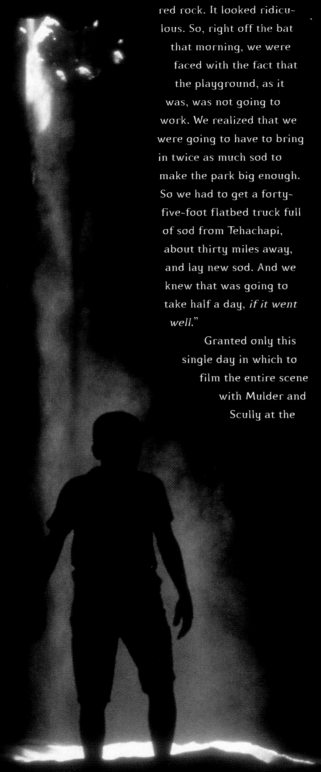

red rock. It looked ridiculous. So, right off the bat that morning, we were faced with the fact that the playground, as it was, was not going to work. We realized that we were going to have to bring in twice as much sod to make the park big enough. So we had to get a forty-five-foot flatbed truck full of sod from Tehachapi, about thirty miles away, and lay new sod. And we knew that was going to take half a day, *if it went well*."

Granted only this single day in which to film the entire scene with Mulder and Scully at the park, Bowman could ill afford to lose half a shooting day. The only way to keep to his schedule was to continue shooting while the new sod was procured, transported, and laid, restaging some of the dialogue between Mulder and Scully so that the small size of the park would not be evident in the frame. The need to restage was something of a disappointment for Bowman, since the originally planned wide shot revealing Mulder and Scully standing in the park, surrounded by the vast desert, had been one of his favorite storyboarded moments. "That scene had been in my mind for months," Bowman said. "It had been planned out carefully, because it was a very important moment in the movie. But suddenly, I was standing in 115 degree heat, my mind racing as I tried to instantly restage a scene that I had worked out carefully two months earlier. I had to figure it out on the spot, as the heat was blowing my brain out of my head. I didn't want the scene to end up looking like I was just winging it, either. So I was trying to think cinematically, trying to figure out how to tell the story visually. The whole day was a matter of pouring cold water on my head, just so I could keep thinking and planning. Until the sun went down, I was examining every shot that I'd just made up on the fly, trying to make sure that the scene flowed and made sense."

The heat, the hot wind, the hurried reconfiguring of the playground set, and the seat-of-the-pants restaging of shots made the last day in California City one of the most trying of the production schedule. "I was wearing a wool suit," recalled Gillian Anderson, "which made the heat just that much worse. And we had hot air blowing in our faces for take after take, until I was actually finding it difficult to breathe. I had to have ice on the back of my neck and in my hands just to keep me cool enough to keep going throughout the afternoon."

The hot, windy weather conditions also created problems for the camera crew. "The wind would come up and blow everything around," said Ward Russell, "so we'd get dirt in the shots where we didn't want it; and then when we did want it, we couldn't get it because the wind would be blowing in the wrong direction." The wind also played havoc with the camera crane, making it bounce and sway inappropriately.

After the desert shoot wrapped on Wednesday evening, the exhausted company moved to Soledad Canyon, another remote exterior location, situated about an hour north of Los

opposite: Kids digging in the desert of a Dallas suburb lead to the discovery of a cave. **left:** When one of the boys, Stevie (Lucas Black) falls into the cave, his body is infiltrated by a black, oily fluid—the conduit of the alien virus.

full spread: Early concept sketch illustrating Stevie's fall into the Texas cave.

Angeles. Filmed in the area were a variety of night scenes that take place as Mulder and Scully pursue mysterious tanker trucks seen leaving the cave site, including shots of the characters atop a bluff that overlooks a cornfield, medium shots of the characters running out of the cornfield, a scene near a railroad crossing, and shots of a tanker-loaded train entering a tunnel.

Although the isolated, rocky canyon provided a wonderful visual backdrop for all of the Texas flatland scenes, the logistics of filming there were nightmarish. One small, narrow road was the only way in or out of the canyon, which made it difficult to transport large-scale equipment to the site. The location was also one of the most difficult to light for Ward Russell, since a very large area of the canyon had to be illuminated sufficiently to film the night scenes. "We had to light a vast area," said Russell. "We broke the work up into first unit and second unit, with first unit shooting all of the stuff with the actors, and second unit filming shots of their car driving by and the train going into the tunnel. I designed all of the lighting schemes for both. The biggest setup was for a shot of the train crossing in one direction as the camera panned through it and aimed in the opposite direction, toward the bluff, which was a long distance away. It was almost a half a mile from one

end of that pan to the other, and we had to light all of it. It took a lot of very big lights." The lighting inventory included two Musco lights—the largest portable lighting units available—a two-hundred-foot condor crane equipped with a bank of 18K and 16K HMIs, and two 150-foot condors, each with a complement of 6K HMIs. With each 6K instrument representing 10,000 watts, the massive lighting setup blasted hundreds of thousands of watts of light onto the area.

The characters' point of view from the bluff also had to be well lit, even though the actual view from that vantage point would be replaced with a cornfield that would be shot the following week in Bakersfield. To enable the visual effects team to matte-in the cornfield, a large blue screen had to be hung from a crane and positioned over the bluff. "Night exteriors are always difficult blue screen situations," noted Mat Beck. "We had to throw a lot of light on the blue screen to ensure we'd be able to pull our matte." Once on location, an unplanned shot of Mulder and Scully walking down the bluff was added, and it was soon discovered that the hanging blue screen was too small to accommodate the additional camera movement. "To extend the blue screen, we had to quickly paint pieces of plywood with blue paint and throw them up wherever we needed them."

top left: Although all of the cave interiors would be shot on a set built on stage at Fox, the exterior cave opening was simulated at the location by a fourteen-foot-deep hole, lined with fiberglass. top center and right: The Haz-Mat team led by Dr. Ben Bronschweig takes over the scene at the cave site. opposite: First Assistant Director, Josh McLaglen, directs the landing of the Haz-Mat helicopter.

Despite the challenges of filming night scenes in the remote and nearly inaccessible canyon, cast and crew morale was high all three nights. Temperatures were in the mid-seventies, and the night air remained still and comfortably balmy. "I love nighttime shoots," Anderson noted. "No matter how long I've been up during the day, something kicks in at about eleven o'clock at night. I get a second wind, and I'm as happy as can be. And it was so beautiful and cool out there in that little canyon. I just loved it. I came to life those nights."

While second unit concentrated on shots involving the train at one end of the canyon, first unit completed its slate, including a dialogue between Mulder and Scully when their car reaches a dead-end; a dead-end that, Scully notes, she has encountered too many times with Mulder. The scene is a significant one in the movie because it reveals Scully's disenchantment with what has been a frustrating five-year quest.

"Our train coordinator, Bob Clark, took care of getting the trains we needed for Soledad Canyon," Lata Ryan said. "He was a great guy who wore overalls every single day, just like a real train conductor. All of the trains and tracks in the movie were Amtrak, since the other railroads no longer cooperate with film production." The scene between Mulder and Scully at the railroad crossing was reshot two weeks later, due to a case of laryngitis suffered by Gillian Anderson during the initial Soledad

above: The young actors watch the scene they just shot on a monitor. **above right:** The crew gets ready to film the scene in which Stevie is lifted from the cave. A dummy of Stevie was used in the cryobubble for the scene. **below right:** The crew filmed the Haz-Mat team on location in California City.

Canyon shoot. "There was so much dust in the canyon that night, it just ruined Gillian's voice. So we went back to that same location a few days later to pick up that scene," said Ryan.

Unwanted elements in the background of what was supposed to be rural Texas—urban blights such as a freeway and streetlights—were painted out of the scene digitally in post-production.

By Sunday morning, all of the shots slated for the Soledad Canyon location were in the can. Monday night, July 21, found the company in Bakersfield, where an eight-acre cornfield had been bought out by the production for filming over the next four nights. Location manager Bob Decker found the cornfield months earlier, and had kept a watch on its condition and rate of growth ever since. "We'd been worried that the corn stalks wouldn't be tall enough by the time we came to shoot the scenes," noted Lata Ryan. "But when we checked out the field a few days beforehand, we discovered that the stalks were actually too tall! So we had to stunt their growth by depriving them of water for the remaining days until shooting."

Erected within the field were two bee domes—thirty feet high, ninety feet wide, and one hundred forty feet long—that had been built by the art department. "They were inflatable domes," explained Chris Nowak, "made out of a translucent material. They were lit from inside, which made them look like giant Christmas ornaments out there in the middle of the cornfield at night."

Ward Russell illuminated not only the interior of the domes, but the entire eight-acre area for wide shots of syndicate helicopters chasing Mulder and Scully through the field of corn. "It was over a quarter-mile from the camera position to our bee dome set at the far end of the cornfield," said Russell. "I had to light up that whole quarter-mile area bright enough so

MONDAY, JULY 14: CALIFORNIA CITY

The film company is at this Mojave Desert location to film scenes involving Stevie's fall into the mouth of an ancient—and deadly—cave. At nine o'clock in the morning, the temperature is already nearing one hundred degrees. Crew members wear hats to protect themselves from the relentless desert sun, and the company medic is prepared with ample supplies of sunscreen. Production assistants continuously roam the site, passing out bottles of water.

The landscape is flat and stark, a wide expanse of hardened dirt that ends abruptly at the fence line of a housing development. There are no trees, and little foliage except a smattering of brush and tumbleweeds. The only shade is under a five-foot-square striped awning that is moved from setup to setup, and under which sit the canvas chairs designated with the names of the director, producers, and principal cast members. Those chairs remain unoccupied throughout most of the day, however, as Chris Carter, Rob Bowman, Dan Sackheim, and Lata Ryan attend to a series of crises, big and small. Carter carries a book—*Introducing Kafka*—but an opportunity for reading between setups never materializes.

"We're starting the day as if Stevie has already fallen in the hole," explains Ryan. "The kids have run to get help, and now fire trucks are starting to arrive at the scene. In the next scene, the helicopters are going to land—both the medevac helicopter and the helicopter carrying Bronschweig and his hazardous materials crew. The next thing we know, there are tankers pulling up, along with a whole entourage of cars. We have to get all of those shots today, along with a crane shot that starts on the hole and rises twenty feet in the air as the kids run away."

The area is dotted with fire trucks dressed with Dallas decals, extras portraying concerned bystanders, and a number of performers dressed in full fireman regalia. Actor Gary Grubbs, who is playing Fire Captain Miles Cooles, seeks a moment of shade under the awning, awaiting his call to action. Like nearly every member of the cast, Grubbs has been given only the pages of the script that pertain to his character. "I haven't read a whole script," says Grubbs, "so I'm not sure what is going on in this scene. I won't know what is going on until I see the movie, just like everybody else." Someone "in the know" jokingly offers to tell him the film's plotline—for a price. Grubbs smiles and shrugs. "I'm not sure I *want* to know," he says. "I think I'd rather be surprised." A character actor whose face has become increasingly familiar in recent years, Grubbs is a veteran of *The X-Files,* having played a small-town sheriff in "Our Town," an episode directed by Rob Bowman. "I had a lot of fun on that episode with Rob, so I was happy to do this movie. Rob had me in to read, and he hired me to do this part of the fireman from Texas. I'm from Mississippi, but I can do Texas for 'em. Most people can't hear the difference, anyway."

As the morning wears on and the temperature rises, shooting shifts from the firemen entering the cave to shots of the medevac helicopter approaching the site and landing. With each take, the helicopter serves to make a bad situation worse by blowing dust and dirt into the air. The dust storm continues, unabated, for several minutes with the rotation of the chopper's blades. Crew members tie bandannas over their mouths and noses, cowboy style. Some wear protective eye gear. After several takes, everyone within a radius of a hundred feet is covered with a half-inch layer of desert grime. The dirt is imbedded in every pore, in the teeth and eyes, caked to the scalp, forming a grimy glue on skin that has been generously slathered with sunscreen. By mid-morning, the entire crew is hot, thirsty, and filthy … and the day is still very young.

opposite: Concept illustrations and the final set for the exterior of Bronschweig's camp at the dig site. **above:** The Cigarette-Smoking Man (William B. Davis) arrives to inspect Bronschweig's setup.

that we could photograph the helicopter action sequence at night. Four Musco lights and two xenons gave us just barely enough light to do what we had to do." Xenon lights were also mounted on the helicopters themselves, aimed toward the field like searchlights. "It fit the plot point of these helicopters looking for the characters on the ground; but those searchlights also became our primary lighting sources." To ensure the black helicopters would show up in the night sky, their rotor blades were painted with white stripes. "The stripes at least allowed us to see circles in the sky as the blades rotated."

The bright lighting necessary to capture the action sequence created plates that were too brightly lit for the purposes of the visual effects crew, who would be compositing clean images of the cornfield—without the actors or helicopters—into the blue screen area of the footage shot from the bluff in Soledad Canyon. As a distant night background, the cornfield should have looked fairly dark. "We were really just stealing those shots for our backgrounds," said Mat Beck, "so, of course, they weren't lit with our needs in mind. And there wasn't time to relight the whole thing just for our shots. No one was going to sit around and wait with a first-unit crew while the visual effects guys relit the cornfield for the background of an effects shot. So I just shot it at a whole range of different exposures, knowing we'd have to play around with the brightness levels once we got to the compositing stage."

Among the difficulties of the Bakersfield shoot was flying the helicopters low enough to the field to actually see them in the frame, without creating a safety hazard for the pilots, actors, and the ground crew—a critical balance orchestrated by aerial coordinator David Paris. Another potential safety hazard was the atmospheric layer of smoke, generated by Paul Lombardi's special effects unit, that covered the entire area. "We needed almost a half-square mile of smoke," Lombardi commented, "and it had to be at a consistent level throughout the area. It also had to be consistent over the course of the three or four days we were filming. We had smoke generators set up and big wind machines to direct it. The difficulty was the wind, which would come up and blow the smoke this way and that. Just when we would finally have it looking right, the wind would come up and ruin it. Smoke isn't one of the real glamorous special effects, but it is actually one of the most difficult things we do."

right: A park hastily erected over the dig site was created by the art department and greens crews, which laid down sod and set up playground equipment on location overnight. When the size of the playground appeared insufficient against the vast surrounding desert, additional sod was quickly procured and laid down out of frame as Rob Bowman continued to shoot close-up and medium shots.

above: Mulder and Scully, unconvinced by the official story of a Hanta virus breakout, arrive to inspect the dig site, but find only the suspiciously new and incongruous park. **right:** Behind the scenes with Gillian Anderson on the set at California City.

leaves, which were very sharp on
ally sliced a couple of times. Ther
which was very uncomfortable. V
David was running ahead of me,
time I caught up to him, the stalk
spring back, whacking me in the

Though no one knew it at tl
Duchovny were not the only peo
teenager, carrying a video camer
aged to sneak into the field and
stalks of corn. From his vantage
teenager videotaped the actors i
domes, and later sold his footage
were shocked to turn on the new
secret set and all of this footage
recalled script supervisor Tricia F
tion, and how we were set up the
have crawled more than a mile t
footage, and that cornfield was

"The funny thing," added B
footage he had caught was really
point of view. The kid had a grea
was hiding in the corn. We were
use his stuff in the movie."

When the scenes with the a
cornfield was set on fire and film
montage of evidence being destr
To help the corn burn more easil
field had been disengaged ten da
with the crop dried out, the corn
like trying to burn celery," recall
charged with burning the field. "
pump about fifteen hundred gall
Then we laid in about a thousanc
whole thing on fire." The burning

opposite: Mulder consults a map when he
search for the mysterious tanker trucks.

designated originally as a day exterior, to tie in with the simultaneous review board hearing scene near the end of the film. But, due to delays in getting the field to burn, day had turned to night by the time the shots were filmed. It was a fortuitous turn of events since, ultimately, the filmmakers decided that the burning cornfield looked more interesting against the night sky than it would have in daylight.

The night shoot in Bakersfield continued through Wednesday morning, after which the production crew returned to downtown Los Angeles, where a building had been located for the exterior of Mulder's Washington, D.C. apartment. There, shots of Scully being taken away by ambulance—after being stung by a bee in the hallway outside Mulder's apartment—and the scene in which Mulder is shot by the bogus ambulance driver were filmed on Thursday, July 24, with the following nights devoted to other city exteriors.

When filming wrapped early in the morning on Sunday, July 27, the company had completed its first round of location shooting. While the location work was hard on the cast and crew, Chris Carter—temporarily freed from the tyranny of his television writing and producing schedule—found the location experience to be something of a vacation. "We worked long days," Carter conceded, "but then we went to our hotel rooms and slept for eight hours. And when we got up, we had three or four hours before we had to be to the set, during which we could read or walk or eat, things I didn't get to do when we were on the lot, because I had to run back to the office to do my other work for the television show. Luckily, I had Frank Spotnitz back in Los Angeles, running things and working with the show's writers so that I could go on location and pay attention to the movie."

The incongruity of the crop in the middle of this rocky canyon is made even more pointed by a large helium-filled lighting balloon that hovers eerily over the patch of green. "We're using this thing as our fill light," notes director of photography Ward Russell, "which will allow us to get right up over the top of the actors during the scene. It is actually a helium balloon, with a light source inside of it. It is tied off right now, but when we shoot, we'll have crew people on the ropes, raising and lowering the balloon, as needed. The idea is that it gives you an easily maneuverable light source. You can't use it in a windy situation, because it'll blow around. But it is great for a still environment like this one. It would have been very difficult to light the actors in this scene any other way."

At one A.M., the light crew mans the ropes as Gillian Anderson and David Duchovny receive some last-minute direction from Rob Bowman. In this shot, Mulder and Scully will emerge from the cornfield, stop to look back at the oncoming helicopters, then turn to run up a hillside toward their rented car. For the sake of continuity, David Duchovny kneels in the dirt to scuff up the knees of his pants, and a member of the wardrobe crew makes tiny cuts in his tie. The makeup crew is asked to "pollinate" the actors, which they do by applying yellowish turmeric to the actors' skin and clothing. Finally, everything is in place, and Bowman rolls his cameras.

Several takes into the shoot, Anderson backs up, prepares to run … and trips over a tumbleweed, falling flat on her back. Concerned, people rush to her aid as she lies on the ground, but the actress herself is in a fit of laughter. "Was that tumbleweed there before?" she asks, between giggles. "How did I miss it all those other times?" She is helped to her feet, and they go again.

With each take, the special effects crew engages large Ritter fans to create a layer of ambient dust, supposedly kicked up by the helicopters that will be inserted into the shots later. Production manager David Womark and second assistant director Michael Moore go over the effects department's needs for the following night of filming.

"How many Ritters are we running tomorrow?" Moore asks.

"What do you mean by 'Ritter'?" Womark counters. "There's a bunch of different kinds of fans, but they're not all Ritters."

"Okay," Moore says, after a brief pause. "How many big-ass fans are we running tomorrow?"

"Four," Womark replies.

✗ FRIDAY JULY 18: SOLEDAD CANYON

After two days of shooting in California City, the crew is readjusting to nights in Soledad Canyon, near Santa Clarita, California, where they are shooting Mulder and Scully's discovery of the cornfield and bee domes from atop a bluff in rural Texas. The bluff actually looks out over the remote rocky canyon, but a cornfield scheduled for filming the following week will ultimately be composited into the scene.

At the bottom of the canyon, a small version of the cornfield—twenty-five-feet-square—has been set up by the art department and greens crews, each separate stalk of real corn plugged into a shallow hole dug in the ground. The mini-cornfield is for close-up and medium shots of Mulder and Scully running through the field as they are chased from the area by mysterious black helicopters—although the helicopters themselves and other wide shots will not be filmed until production moves to its larger cornfield location in Bakersfield.

opposite: The agents' pursuit of the tankers leads them to a giant cornfield, inhabited by strange, glowing bee domes. Concept illustrations reveal the domes as seen from a bluff, an early visualization of the dome exterior, and the dome interior.

IV THE SHOOT: ON STAGE

With production entering a month-long period of shooting on the stages at Fox, Carter's "vacation" was over. Season five of *The X-Files* would be going into production in less than a month, requiring Carter to devote more of his attention to the show. "I was writing three of the first five episodes during that period," Carter said, "so my days were really full. Once I was in the thick of it, I was writing twelve hours a day, out of necessity. I bring a real blue-collar ethic to writing. So much of it is just sitting your butt in a chair and putting your fingers on the keyboard and not getting up until it is done. You have to have talent, of course, and you have to have good ideas, and you have to be a writer. But there are a lot of people out there who have all of those qualities, and yet, they don't produce anything because they don't have the discipline."

Several locations would be revisited at the end of the schedule, when sequences that did not feature Mulder and Scully would be shot; but for the following month, the cast and crew settled onto the Fox lot. The logistics of filming onstage were simpler, the work was closer to home, and body clocks were able to reset themselves after the long period of disorienting night shooting. The downside was that, within the controlled confines of sound-stages, the length of work days would no longer be determined by the rising and setting of the sun. Days could go on as long as the overtime budget allowed.

Monday, July 28, was a planning day for Chris Carter, Rob Bowman, Dan Sackheim, Lata Ryan, and fifty members of the crew, as they prepared for the upcoming two-week shoot on the film's largest and most complex set, the interior of the spaceship on Stage 16. "We'd all walked through the set before," Carter noted, "but that Monday was the first day we'd seen it with pre-lighting and the cryopods. It was a big day." On the agenda that day was the planning of spaceship interior shots, among the most exacting on the schedule, due to the fact that only a small percentage of the massive spaceship interior had actually been built onstage. All but the tightest shots of the spaceship interior would require computer-generated imagery. "Every time the camera panned up or off that set, a CG shot was going to be required to complete the image. So we had to figure out where to hang green screens—the area the CG shots would be matted into—and how to frame each shot so that we didn't wind up needing more CG shots than we'd storyboarded and budgeted."

Preparations continued on Stage 16 as first unit picked up with a scene between Mulder and the Well-Manicured Man in the limousine interior on Tuesday, July 29. Rather than film the moving car in the city, the limousine was set up on a rear-projection stage, with background city imagery projected to appear outside

opposite: Night shooting in a cornfield in Bakersfield included low-flying helicopters intended to chase Mulder and Scully from the project site. **top and bottom:** Bowman and Duchovny review takes on a video monitor in Bakersfield. **center:** The dangerous low-flying helicopter maneuvers were coordinated by David Paris. Mulder and Scully spot the approaching helicopters.

the windows of the car. The production had attempted to find stock footage of Washington, D.C. for the rear projection setup; but when no appropriate footage was found, freelance director of photography Dave Drzewiecki was hired to drive around Los Angeles one night, shooting backgrounds. "That footage became our rear-projection plate for the windows of the limousine," explained Mat Beck. "The stage wasn't long enough for the projection throw we needed, so we had to mount our screen on a truck outside the stage to get the right distance. Rear-projection is old-fashioned, but it is still a good way to go for some shots. You can get a perfectly good effect with it, especially for night shots." Once the car and rear projector were set up, Duchovny and John Neville were brought in to perform the scene, with Rob Bowman directing. "It was so much better than trying to do it out in a real car, in the middle of town. The sound quality was much better because we were onstage, for one thing. Everything was more controlled."

Wednesday, July 30 saw Chris Carter stepping behind the second-unit cameras to direct a morgue scene in which Scully— having performed her autopsy on the fireman's remains— attempts to avoid detection by security personnel as she engages in the inevitable cell phone conversation with Mulder.

Although the scene had been designated for the first-unit shoot originally, it was relegated to Carter and a second-unit crew as a means of catching up on time lost the previous Saturday, when Gillian Anderson's voice had gone out due to a case of laryngitis. In a classic case of "turnaround is fair play," Rob Bowman, at work on another stage, frequently took time between setups to check on Carter's progress.

"Rob was always joking about my tapping him on the back while he was directing, giving him my input," Carter said. "So when I was directing this second-unit sequence, he'd come in and say, 'Don't worry. I'm not going to tap on your back.' But he did stand behind me at times, and I could feel his presence. Rob is a stickler for composition, and I wanted to make sure I made him happy. I printed a couple more of everything because I wanted to give him the opportunity to choose from a variety of takes, rather than be forced to take my choice. Overall, the day went well. I had directed Gillian before, and I knew the scene well. And Rob and Ward Russell, the DP, were just a few steps away, so they were available if I had any questions about the lighting or the scene. In that regard, it was training-wheels time."

While Carter shot the second-unit morgue scene that Wednesday, Rob Bowman and the first-unit crew were making their way through the first day of filming on the interior spaceship set on Stage 16, the setting for a long sequence in which Mulder explores the ship interior, frees Scully from the cryopod, and encounters an alien that has burst from a host body as the temperature inside the ship rises. The massive greenish colored structure on Stage 16 had been the most chal-

above left: The Well-Manicured Man (John Neville) meets clandestinely with Mulder to give him crucial information about the Project, as well as the coordinates of where Scully is being held and a vaccine against the alien virus with which she is infected. **opposite:** Mulder watches in shock as the Well-Manicured Man's car explodes.

enging of all the set designs, and its completion in time for filming had required a Herculean effort from both the art department and construction crews. "Designing the spaceship interior was a big job, right off the bat," said Chris Nowak, "because the script was very vague about what it should look like. The action in the script moved from one nondescript area to another, never pinpointing what each of those areas represented. In a very short time frame, we had to develop the exact look of this set, revising concepts as the script changed or Rob's storyboards changed. It had to be designed fast if there was going to be even a possibility of getting it built in time."

As scripted, neither Mulder nor the audience would be aware that the cavernous space was actually the interior of an alien spacecraft until later in the sequence, when Mulder and Scully—having climbed their way back up to the ice field—witness the ship's rise and subsequent takeoff. "We tried to keep the set mysterious looking," Nowak asserted. "We wanted it to look otherworldly and bizarre, so that the people in the audience wouldn't know what they were looking at."

The set was finally designed as a series of huge tubular structures, leading down to corridors lined with cryopods. Initially, the plan had been to build a separate set for each main area of the ship. But when the movie's budget failed to accommodate such a grand scheme, the ship was designed and built as one giant set, flexible enough to contain all of the action in the script. "We had to combine all of those different sets into one big set," said Nowak, "taking out walls as needed, or redressing areas to make them look different as Mulder moved from one area of the ship to another. We had to come up with ways to make this one set do double, triple and quadruple duty." Construction on the set, which would take up every inch of the massive soundstage, began just eight weeks prior to the start of filming in the spaceship interior. "The set was made up of layers of plaster, foam, and styrene. Building it was a lot of work. Our crews worked on it for sixty days straight, without a break, in order to get it done in time."

While the art department and construction crews were

opposite: Syndicate elders meet to discuss the mutating alien virus at a men's club in Kensington, England. Interiors for the scene were shot in a faculty club at the California Institute of Technology in Pasadena. **below:** Scully infiltrates a hospital morgue to examine the remains of one of the bombing victims. **inset:** Scully performs her clandestine autopsy on the dead fireman, whose body was infected by the alien virus.

one corridor were built by an outside vendor, then delivered to the stage. Host bodies seen inside the green-glowing cryopods were built by ADI and KNB. The former created two mechanical, articulated host bodies that would be featured in the sequence in which aliens begin hatching and breaking free of the cryopods—one victim recognizable as the primitive who was infected with the alien virus in the movie's opening scene, and another in an equally advanced stage of infection. Both articulated bodies were made of transparent silicone, supported by a core that represented what little is left of the host's internal organs and bone structure. "The alien inside uses the host's proteins and organs to feed itself," explained Alec Gillis. "So as the embryo grows, the body withers and becomes nothing but a husk."

Seen clearly through the transparent bodies were the full-term aliens that would burst from the hosts and break free of the ice-encased cryopod during the hatching sequence. Rather than build two all-new articulated alien puppets for the hatching shots, ADI modified the postpartum creature head and suit that would be worn by Tom Woodruff, and fit them into the articulated hosts. "We made a little stuffed version of the suit by taking in darts and tucks," explained Woodruff, "and put that inside the transparent host body. To allow for facial expression as the creature broke free, we positioned our hero articulated head inside the body as well. If you pulled the whole thing out of the body, it looked very silly: a big head on a tiny, atrophied body. But it worked when it was all tucked and folded into this human host organism. It was a huge cheat, but it served to complete the illusion for the audience." Facial articulation in the creature's head was radio-controlled from off-camera; but gross body movement as the alien struggled to be born was accomplished without mechanical means. "We found the best way to do it was just to let the puppeteers hide behind the cryopod, reach into the window in the back of the host body, and move the creature around with their hands. That was enough movement to make the creature seem alive."

Background cryopods that would not be featured in the hatching sequence were inhabited by non-mechanical prop bodies created by KNB. "The production needed generic host bodies," explained Howard Berger, "revealing two stages of alien infection. We built five males and five females for the first-stage hosts, which were just normal-looking, frozen bodies. Then we built four second-stage bodies—two males and two females—which were transparent and bloated, with the creature clearly inside. None of these bodies had to be mechanical, because they weren't going to be seen in any of the shots of the alien break-

ing out. They were essentially props, but they had to be really good-looking props. My thinking was that, even if the audience never saw the level of detail in these bodies, Chris Carter and Rob Bowman would. I knew they would be on the set, inspecting these bodies up close. I wanted them to look good for Chris and Rob, if no one else."

The first-stage background bodies were either free-sculpted or made from generic lifecasts KNB had on hand from previous projects. Final bodies were made of silicone, backed with polyurethane foam, then painted. Clear silicone was used for the four second-stage bodies, fitted with alien embryos made of foam latex. "We over-painted the foam creature so that it would show up clearly through the host skin," said Berger. "We also helped the visibility by making the silicone super-thin in the stomach area." When the foam embryos still did not show up clearly enough through the skin, Berger and his crew removed the 3-D props and simply painted the embryo shape onto the vacuformed core inside the transparent host bodies.

The most recognizable of the first-stage victims is Agent Scully, comatose and frozen within the life-sustaining cryopod. KNB was charged with providing the nude likeness of Gillian Anderson, created from the actress's own head cast and a body cast taken from a double. Anderson—who had undergone the head cast process once before for the television show—dreaded going through the experience again for the film. "I tend to be claustrophobic anyway," Anderson explained. "It is pretty horrible to be covered with the casting material. The worst part is that everything goes quiet once they cover up your ears. You hear nothing, you see nothing, and you can only breathe through these little straws. I found it to be a really terrifying experience the first time around. Fortunately, when they did the head cast for the movie, it went much more quickly than it had before."

"Gillian was great to work with," said Berger. "She was a little wary about the head cast, but it went very smoothly and she was very cooperative. And the body prop turned out beautifully."

Dressed with the cryopods and their host occupants, the completed spaceship interior filled the entire soundstage. But as massive as the final set was, it represented only a small percentage of the entire spacecraft interior. The remaining levels and areas of the ship would be computer generated by Mat Beck's digital effects team at Light Matters. These digital set extensions would be matted into background areas of the set, which were draped with green screen material to accommodate the postproduction process.

In the days leading up to the interior spaceship shoot, a rigging crew had hung the green screens from the stage ceiling on a rail-type rig that would allow them to swing the material into position, as needed. Beck had determined that green would be the most suitable matting color, due to the color of the set, the predominantly blue light Ward Russell had used to illuminate the set during tests, and the blue color of the suit that would be worn by David Duchovny in the sequence. Since the digital matting technique relies on the computer's ability to recognize and pinpoint a specific color, the heavily featured blue in the lights, set, and wardrobe ruled out using blue-screen. But as the shoot progressed, Beck and his team found themselves hurriedly setting up blue screen and even red screen material for specific shots. "Once we got to actual filming," explained Beck, "the predominant lighting color changed from blue to green, which was going to make it much harder to pull a green-screen matte. I was worried about it; and at one point, I approached Chris Carter and said, 'Uh, isn't this lighting awfully green?' Chris responded, 'Yeah—and I like it.' And, of course, there was nothing to say, except: 'Yeah, boy, me too. I surely like that green lighting.'" The glowing green color of the cryopods complicated the situation even more. "Suddenly,

I had the worst possible scenario: blue clothing on the actor in the scene, but green lighting and green cryopods. We ended up having to choose our matte color shot by shot, and in some cases, area by area within a single shot." Blue screen was used when the green cryopods were being filmed, while green screen was used when Duchovny's blue suit was in the shot. "We just put green where we had to and blue where we had to, mixing and matching them as needed." A third matte color, red, was used for tracking markers placed around the set, markers that would enable the digital team to match the movement of its virtual camera to that of the live-action camera. "We had these reference cubes painted Day-Glo red so that they would contrast against the green, against the blue, and also against the foreground."

Before Beck and his crew ever got to the set, the digital set extensions had been carefully previsualized in rough CG animatics. "It was really important that we do previsualizations," said Beck, "because some of these set extension shots were very complicated. We had to work out camera moves beforehand, and work out where we were going to need blue or green for every move that the camera made. The previz stuff was also very helpful in giving everyone an idea of what the final shots

Weeks prior to the shoot on the spaceship interior, Beck and his team prepared computer generated previsualizations for each of the visual effects shots in the sequence. Even with that preparation, however, there is some uncertainty on the set this morning, some doubt as to exactly where the camera should be positioned and how a pan of Mulder carrying Scully through the ship corridor should be framed. Although similar shots had been storyboarded and previsualized, this exact pan—which will start on the live-action set and end on the live-action set, but will incorporate a wide shot of the digital spaceship in between—was not on the agenda until today. "It always happens," Beck says, philosophically. "You always wind up doing shots that you're not prepared for and that weren't planned in advance. So we're scrambling a little bit right now. We're throwing up a blue screen to accommodate this unplanned-for shot; and if it isn't perfect, we'll be able to deal with that at the other end, when we're compositing these plates with the CG part of the set. One of the virtues of digital technology is that it can accommodate changes more easily than other types of visual effects."

Later in the day, the crew prepares to shoot the final leg of Mulder's climb down from the top of the spaceship interior to the corridor where Scully is encased in a cryopod. Wearing a parka and holding a flashlight,

THURSDAY, JULY 31: INTERIOR SPACESHIP

It is just after nine o'clock in the morning. Visual effects supervisor Mat Beck has been on the set since seven, preparing upcoming wide shots of the spaceship interior, into which his team will be compositing digital set extensions. "The first thing I had to do today was talk with the overnight riggers," Beck says. "A shot that was scheduled to go tomorrow is going today, instead, so we had the overnight riggers hanging lights for our massive green and blue screens. The schedule keeps changing, so we're really tap dancing to keep one step ahead of the game. This is a complex, ambitious movie, and we're trying to get a lot done in a very short amount of time. But we're all committed to making this stuff look terrific, despite everything."

Duchovny jumps into frame from the middle section of an off-camera ladder to suggest Mulder's final drop into the corridor. Just as cameras are about to roll, script supervisor Tricia Ronten reminds attending crew members to turn on Duchovny's flashlight.

On the next take, Bowman asks Duchovny if he would be comfortable dropping from the top of the ladder, rather than the middle, to make the jump more dynamic. "I'd be comfortable with that," Duchovny assures him. The actor climbs to the top of the ladder and positions himself atop one of the set's tubular structures. Just prior to "action," a crew member hastily removes the ladder, leaving Duchovny hanging for a moment before he drops from the height and into frame. Bowman seems happy with this take, and the crew sets up for Mulder's subsequent search of the corridor.

would look like, which was important, since so much of the spaceship interior was going to be CG. The set area represented only about 1/32nd of that ship. The other 31/32nds were going to be generated in the computer. So not only did the previsualizations help me determine where the camera was going to be and where the green screen or blue screen needed to be, they helped everyone on the set see what the shots were going to look like once the CG set extensions were added."

Despite the previsualizations and the planning efforts the previous Monday, the first day of filming the spaceship interior was characterized by some anxiety and an overall uncertainty as to how shots should be framed or how the camera should move through the space. That anxiety was well founded. Every time the camera moved off the immediate set, a digital set extension would have to be composited into the shot, and, because computer-generated shots are extremely expensive, only a limited number had been budgeted. "It was another example of how our short prep time had a big impact on the production," Chris Carter noted. "We should have had weeks and weeks to plan out those shots. Instead, Rob was suddenly plopped onto this set, with very little preparation. And as soon as he started to shoot, he was being told that he couldn't put his camera where he wanted it to go. Mat had done wonderful previsualizations for the sequence; but until we actually got a camera on the set, in the physical environment, we couldn't truly imagine everything that the camera was going to see."

Fast thinking and on-the-fly shot designs were required throughout the interior spaceship shoot. "We wound up doing a lot of seat-of-the-pants stuff on that set," Beck admitted. "Everybody was scrambling. Rob was improvising shots; we were throwing up green screens as fast as we could. We had to solve things so quickly, I shot some of the funkiest blue screen and green screen stuff of my career for this show. But the digital guys I work with had saved my butt before and I had faith that they would again. Principal photography is too expensive to waste time trying to get an absolutely perfect visual effects setup. It was a point of pride with us that first unit never had to wait for a green screen shot, in spite of the fact that we were making them up as we went along."

Mulder's climb down from the entrance at the top of the ship interior to the cryopod corridors below was scheduled for

opposite: An abductee is very visible behind the thick ice covering of the cryopod.

control mechanisms for moving the creature's eyes, lips, cheeks, and brows had to be fitted into a five-inch space within the head. "There were also radio receivers and batteries packed inside the head," said Tom Woodruff. "All of the radio control articulations were operated by three puppeteers on joystick controls." Less complex mechanically, the stunt attack head was cable-operated. "It had a double-hinged jaw in it; and through the cable, we could drop that jaw down, opening the mouth much wider than the hero head was capable of doing."

The creature heads and suits were worn by Woodruff, who had performed a number of creature roles for films such as *Leviathan*, *Jumanji*, *Alien³* and *Alien Resurrection*. Positioned over Woodruff's own skull, the creature head added another four inches of height to the performer's six-foot, two-inch frame, making the alien nearly six-feet, six-inches tall. "They wanted this to be a tall, powerful creature," noted Woodruff, "something that looked like it actually could tear apart a couple of cavemen. If he were only four feet tall, like the classic gray, would he really be able to overpower these guys? They didn't want a small, scrabbling, screeching little alien. They wanted something much more imposing." While the head interior allowed just enough room for the requisite mechanisms, no space remained for a window or small video monitor to aid Woodruff's vision. "In my past creature work, I've always had some way of seeing out of the mechanical heads. But since we didn't have room for either a window or a video screen in this head, I was basically blind when I was inside of it." Unable to see, Woodruff relied on his memory of the set layout as he performed each scene, as well as on guidance and cues from his off-camera crew.

the first few days in the spaceship interior, followed by his rescue of Scully from the cryopod. Several days on the set would also be devoted to capturing the first footage of the alien as it hatched from its cryogenically maintained host and pursued Mulder and Scully through the ship interior. While aliens had been featured in several episodes of *The X-Files*, the movie would serve as the audience's introduction to this particular creature. "This alien could be considered a relative of the grays we've seen in the TV episodes," said Rob Bowman, "just as gorillas are related to human beings. But this specific alien had never been seen in the television show."

Built by ADI, primitive and modern versions of the alien were conceived through a series of drawings and three-dimensional maquettes before undergoing construction. Both versions required two separate heads each: an articulated hero head, and a stunt head, sculpted in a fierce expression, with its brows lowered and its jaws opened wide, specifically for attack scenes. All of the heads consisted of support underskeletons, covered with foam latex "skins." On the hero versions, all of the radio

above left: Filming on the set of the spaceship interior. **below:** Mulder watches anxiously as Scully climbs the vent to escape the alien ship. **opposite:** One of many cryopods built for the interior spaceship sequences.

His role as the creature also required Woodruff to don a foam latex bodysuit, made from a cut-down lifecast of his body to ensure it would be as tight and form-fitting as possible. The foam latex skin—formulated and painted to look like a tough, leathery hide—was attached to a Lycra bodysuit for added strength and support. "Of all the suits I've worn," noted Woodruff, "this one was the tightest. It took a full ten minutes just to work it up over my hips, because we'd made the waist area very small. But, once it was on, it conformed completely to my body, without any wrinkling around the joints. It stretched like a wet suit, taking the form of a second skin, which made the alien body look very natural. It was so tight-fitting, you could actually see my ribs through the suit." Talcum powder sprinkled inside eased the process of getting into the girdle-like suit, which closed through a zipper in the back. After the suit was on, a cowl piece was glued down to the shoulders, covering the zipper and acting as a mantle for the head. Separate feet, pulled over Woodruff's own, completed the transformation.

In addition to the creature heads and bodysuits, a set of mechanical hands were built for insert shots of either the primitive or modern alien attacking. "They weren't attached to anything else," said Woodruff. "They were just for close-ups of the hands during attacks. They were cable-operated by one puppeteer to make the fingers move and the claws extend from the tips of the fingers; and a second puppeteer operated a rod at the elbow and wrist, just to give the whole arm some gross movement."

When all of the creature pieces had been fabricated, Woodruff and Gillis conducted film tests to pin down the choreography of the alien's movements. "I came up with a lot of very quick, bird-like moves," Woodruff revealed, "interspersed with smooth transitional moves to get from one position to another. I tried to keep the movement in one of those two modes—either slow and graceful, or quick and staccato—just to keep it interesting." Those movements were rejected in favor of a much more contained behavioral style, when Bowman and the producers determined that the simpler the performance, the more natural the

opposite: Following Mulder and Scully's climb from the ship, the surrounding ice field begins to implode in giant sheets. The sequence was realized through a combination of stage, location, and miniature photography footage.

alien appeared on screen. "Chris Carter and Rob Bowman weren't happy with the stylized performance, so I dropped that completely. They didn't think it looked natural. Rob and I ended up joking about the creature looking like a *Solid Gold* dancer— something he wanted to avoid, obviously. It was such a thinly disguised human figure, it turned out that the less I did, the more effective it was. Rob's feeling was that, in terms of performance, less was more."

Bowman also took a "less is more" approach to filming the creature. "I took my lead from those that have gone before me," Bowman stated. "Movies like *Jaws*, old black-and-white monster movies, and even German expressionistic films to an exaggerated degree, all let the audiences create the monsters in their own minds. I also looked at the original *Alien* to get some ideas; and I discovered that you hardly see the alien in that movie. You only see flashes of it. I wanted to do the same thing, giving the audience the basic dotted outline of the creature, and then letting them connect the dots. I had a full-blown, head-to-toe creature to work with; but I made sure the audience would never get a really good look at it." Maintaining that minimalist approach

throughout all of the alien scenes required both discipline and imagination on Bowman's part. "The easiest thing would have been to just shoot the thing in full view. But every day I went in determined to hold that tension. The trickiest shots were the ones where he was just standing there, without any frenetic action to hide the fact that it was a performer in a suit. I was also concerned, throughout the entire filming of the movie, that the creature attack scenes would end up looking silly, but they ended up anything but silly. By being very careful in how we shot the creature and how we staged all of those scenes, we wound up with an alien who was an ass-kicker."

Woodruff's first scenes in the suit were those in which the creature crawls through a ventilation duct in pursuit of Mulder and Scully. Since the constricting suit made climbing through the tube nearly impossible, Woodruff laid on a dolly rig and pulled himself through the set with his hands. "It was supposed to be a very frenetic movement through there anyway," said Woodruff, "and this dolly really helped me get up some speed."

While some creature footage was filmed during the second week on the interior spaceship set, most of the alien

---

FRIDAY, AUGUST 1: TEN THIRTEEN PRODUCTIONS

Situated on the Twentieth Century Fox lot, the Ten Thirteen Productions bungalow is small and unpretentious, lacking the glamour of some of the other production companies housed there. Blowups of magazine covers featuring the *X-Files* stars and other printed matter generated by the show's success are framed and mounted on the walls, as are some of the awards it has won over the past four years. The awards are so numerous, however, many have not found a place of honor on the walls, and remain neatly stacked in corners or leaned up against file cabinets.

Much of the space in the bungalow is taken up by Chris Carter's comfortable, well-appointed office. With the movie well into production, Carter's days are divided between the soundstages and this office, where he devotes much of his time to writing episodes for the upcoming season of *The X-Files* or penning revisions to the movie's screenplay—a process that continues, even though the production is about to pass its halfway mark. "I'm still revising the scenes we haven't shot yet," Carter notes. "Some of the changes are production oriented, a matter of 'we can't do this' or 'we can't do this

for the amount of time and money that we have.' Other changes I'm making are just the result of my constantly reevaluating what makes the story work, and what will make it better."

When he is not writing, Carter is attending to his duties both as a producer on the movie and as the television show's executive producer. In terms of producing, Carter has discovered that there is little difference between the two arenas. "I've always thought of the *X-Files* television show as a mini-movie anyway," Carter observes. "And we film the show, so it is actually the same medium. The differences have been minimal. The movie crew is bigger, but not substantially so. There are three-hundred-plus people working on the TV show each and every day, and the movie's crew isn't much bigger than that. The exceptions are the art department and effects crews, which are both bigger, by several times, than what we have on the show. The most significant difference, in terms of production, has been dealing with the size of the movie screen, which demands more time, more money, more detail, and more expertise. There's been the need to do more, and to do it in a larger way."

Though the bungalow that houses Carter's office is the only building with a placard reading TEN THIRTEEN PRODUCTIONS—named for Carter's October 13 birthday—the company, in reality, is spread out over buildings and trailers in the surrounding area. Among those satellite offices is the one belonging to *X-Files* co-executive producer Frank Spotnitz, who is currently working closely with the show's writing staff, overseeing scripts for the upcoming season. As the movie's co-producer, Spotnitz is also keeping tabs on its progress; but with the start of television production fast approaching, the show has become his first priority. "I was very involved with the movie when we were prepping it," Spotnitz explains. "But now that it is actually shooting, I've been put in the role of keeping the television show running so that Chris can be on the movie set, which he has been, every single day."

At one o'clock, both Carter and Spotnitz emerge from their respective offices and walk the distance to a small projection room where dailies will be screened. The screening room—packed with producers and other crew members—is standing room only by the time Carter and Spotnitz arrive. Several people rise to offer their seats, but the men wave them back down, opting to sit cross-legged on the floor.

right: Mulder resuscitates Scully after freeing her from the cryopod.

shots—particularly those involving the creature's breakout from the cryopod—were postponed until later in the schedule, due to a major snag midway through the shoot on Stage 16 when the mechanical cryopods failed to function as planned. "There was a series of storyboards showing exactly how it was supposed to happen," recalled Lata Ryan. "First, the paddles on the pods were supposed to open; then the creature's hands were supposed to break out through the ice; then water from the melted ice was supposed to flow. But when the time came to shoot the sequence, the mechanical paddles didn't open, the simulated ice didn't break away properly, and the water didn't flow. It was a mess."

Dan Sackheim suggested the breakout might be better executed if a powerful set of mechanical creature hands were used for the effect, rather than the foam latex gloves worn by Woodruff. "Dan was concerned that I couldn't make the effect look explosive enough, just using my own strength in these gloved hands," Woodruff explained. "He thought something mechanical might do a better job, and that having a big metal hand break through might be the solution to the breakaway problem." To accommodate Sackheim's request, members of the ADI team worked around the clock to produce the mechanical hands in time for the imminently scheduled reshoot; but the mechanical appendages were never used. "When we attempted the effect again, it became very clear that it was the quality of the simulated ice, not the hand, that made the breakaway effect dynamic or not. So after this big effort to get them done, the hands were never used. But those disappointments are just part of the package when you do this kind of work."

The malfunctioning set pieces also caused major delays in the filming of Mulder's rescue of Scully from the cryopod. "Everyone had underestimated how difficult it was going to be to simulate ice and to create the effect of ice breaking," remarked production manager David Womark. "We'd all thought, 'Oh, no problem. Mulder will just grab something and smash through this thick covering of ice on the cryopod.' It turned out to be much more difficult than that. Just breaking through the ice material was a problem, because it happened too easily at first. It was supposed to be a two-foot-thick layer of ice over the cryopod; and it didn't look realistic to have Mulder break through that too easily. Because of our short prep, we had never worked out how we would break through

opposite: Mulder rescues Scully.

below: Bee dome interiors were filmed on stage at Fox, where bee wrangler Dr. Norman Gary and his crew released 300,000 bees over the course of three days of filming. Crew members shielded themselves with special protective gear. **bottom:** Producer Dan Sackheim and David Duchovny. **opposite:** Mulder and Scully inspect the bee dome interior.

the ice, or how we would get a breakaway material to look like ice, or how we would transition from the Scully dummy in the cryopod to the real Gillian emerging from it. We'd never had the time to test what turned out to be a very difficult gag."

The production was in trouble. With fewer than twenty days left before Duchovny and Anderson had to return to Vancouver, precious little time remained for rebuilding the cryopods so that Mulder's rescue of Scully and his reactions to the hatching alien could be filmed. Looking for a solution that would not delay production, the filmmakers briefly considered shooting Duchovny's reactions to the creature only, then filming the hatching sequence separately, after the actor had returned to Vancouver. The downside of the plan was that the climactic confrontation between Mulder and the alien that had been building throughout the film's narrative—and, in some respects, throughout the five seasons of the show—would have to

be assembled after-the-fact, without benefit of Duchovny and the creature ever having been filmed together in the same frame.

Obviously, it was not the ideal way to create the climax of their movie. "We wanted to figure out a way to let Rob have the creature and Mulder in the scene together," Dan Sackheim recalled. "It was very important because it was the only chance Rob was going to get to have the creature and Mulder actually interacting with each other." An alternate plan was conceived, with Paul Lombardi and his crew assuming the task of rebuilding the cryopods within the following two weeks so that Bowman could take another stab at the scene before the actors' departure. "We rebuilt half a dozen cryopods in two weeks," Lombardi said. "They were made of plastic and fiberglass over aluminum frames, and they were fully articulated with pneumatic rams to open the flipper paddles." Breakaway material was positioned in different areas of the cryopod, depending on the action assigned to that pod. "Each cryopod had a different requirement: a creature head had to come through one; an arm came through another; a whole body came through another. We used acrylic plastics that we vacuformed into various shapes,

below: An emotional moment between Mulder and Scully in the hallway outside Mulder's apartment when Scully comes to tell Mulder that she is resigning from the FBI. **opposite:** Gillian Anderson has her makeup touched up.

and intermingled those pieces with the breakaway material to create a half-inch-thick covering that looked like ice."

The cryopod calamity had necessitated a juggling of the shooting schedule; and on Monday, August 11, two days earlier than planned, the crew moved to the interior of the bee dome on Stage 6. The translucent, parachute-like set—one of two that had been filmed in Bakersfield—was the setting for the scene in which Mulder and Scully are chased out of the dome by a swarm of bees. Because filming in the bee dome interior had been pushed up on the schedule, preparations were hurried. Among the precautions taken beforehand was the screening of cast and crew members for bee sting allergies. While neither Duchovny nor Anderson tested positively, Anderson's stunt double was found to be allergic, and had to be replaced for this one scene's stunt work.

The 300,000 bees released inside the dome over the course of three days—one first unit and two second unit—were wrangled by entomologist Dr. Norman Gary, who arrived the previous Friday to test the conditions within the inflated set. Over the weekend, the bees were kept in four beehives in a staging area just outside the dome, and were transported to the set in small screened cages when it came time to shoot on Monday. "When they were needed for action," said Gary, "we would shake them through an opening in the cage, into a plastic tray. Then I would run through the dome with this tray, scooping out bees with a little scooper, as needed. Sometimes I would use the scoop to gently sculpt the bees onto the actors, creating a nice layer of bees on them. When we needed flying bees, I would scoop them up quickly and toss them into the air, and they would automatically take wing. We'd have as many as twenty thousand bees at a time, flying around Scully and Mulder as they ran through this cloud of bees." To make the swarm on the characters look even thicker, dead bees were collected at the end of the day and glued onto the actors' costumes. (After spending an entire day engaged in the unpleasant task of gluing dead bees onto costumes, the wardrobe crew returned to the wardrobe trailer the next day to find thousands of ants feasting on the dead insects.)

After filming with the principals on Monday, the following two days were spent shooting wider shots of the stunt doubles running through the bee swarm. "When they reached the end of the dome," said Gary, "the bees were blown off of them with big fans set up by the special effects people. I had told them that a bee can cling to something even with a fifty-mile-per-hour wind blowing on it; and, frankly, I didn't think they'd be able to blow these bees off with fans. But they set up a really good system, and it worked perfectly." The special effects team also provided five-by-five-foot, remote-controlled mechanical units used for insert shots of the bees entering the dome interior through a series of louvers.

Though most members of the crew, the stunt doubles, and the actors worked without protective clothing throughout the three-day shoot, only a handful of people were stung. "None of the actors or stunt doubles were stung," David Womark reported, "even though they were all swarmed with bees. We used Off on them, and I think that helped." The worst casualty of the bee shoot was Dan Sackheim, who had refused all protective gear in

TUESDAY, AUGUST 12: MULDER'S APARTMENT

After the logistical nightmares of shooting locations, intricate spaceship interiors, and bee swarms, the crew is enjoying a much-needed respite on Stage 11, where a scene within Mulder's apartment is being shot. Featuring no special effects, no big camera moves, no special lighting setups, and no visual effects shots, the intimate scene is being filmed by a small crew. It is quiet and calm on stage. Voices are subdued. People walk, rather than run. David Duchovny sits in a chair just outside the flats that make up the walls of his character's apartment, reading a film industry trade paper.

"Today we're shooting the scene where Scully comes to Mulder's apartment and tells him that she is resigning," explains first assistant director Josh McLaglen. "There's almost a lethargic feeling on the set. Everybody is a little tired, a little passive, just because it is a much easier day—a small scene on a simple set on stage. We've been working six-day weeks for quite a while now, so the fatigue is definitely starting to set in. We're all exhausted. But we're getting there. By the end of this week, we will have finished fifty out of seventy-two days."

Even on this laid-back day, McLaglen's radio crackles frequently with questions from crew members at work on other stages. But like all first assistant directors—the logistical engineers of movie production—McLaglen is accustomed to working under pressure. And for all of its

challenges, the *X-Files* movie has been easier than some. "Before this show," McLaglen says, "I was on *Titanic,* which was a really long, exhausting shoot. This film has been, in some ways, a real nice break. We're working on the lot; it is a short, 72-day schedule; and these are all really nice people." His radio squawks with the news that his attention is needed immediately on Stage 15, where construction and rigging crews are preparing the exterior spaceship set for the start of filming there on Thursday. McLaglen leaves the relative serenity of Stage 11 to tackle yet another problem.

As lights are set up around the ten-by-fifteen-foot apartment living room set, Duchovny throws a softball with a crew member nearby. Their game of catch is interrupted when the set is lit satisfactorily; and Duchovny takes his place at a small desk, where, as Fox Mulder, he looks through the pages of a family photo album, in search of a photo of a young Dr. Kurtzweil. His musings are interrupted by the arrival of Scully, who has come to tell him of her decision to resign from the FBI.

The scene is played so intimately, so quietly, the actors' dialogue cannot be clearly heard, even from a distance of only ten feet, where Rob Bowman, Chris Carter, and Dan Sackheim watch the scene on a monitor and listen to the words through headphones.

When ten takes have been shot, Duchovny joins the filmmakers at the monitor, giving them his input as the takes are run, one by one. He particularly likes take 8, and asks for that one to be printed. As the playback continues, the filmmakers review a moment in which Mulder says, "We are *close* to something here, Scully." Duchovny announces, "That's a trailer moment. 'We are *close* to something here, Scully'—cut to spaceship." Carter smiles and nods in agreement.

a gesture of solidarity with the actors, and was stung not once, but multiple times, making his ear swell noticeably.

Up front, the prospect of the bee shoot had been an unappealing one, due to the crew's anxiety about working in an enclosed space with 300,000 bees. "People are irrationally afraid of bees," Gary noted. "They think they are allergic to them, when they're not. On every movie set, I have to calm people down and reassure them that there is no risk in working with bees. It's funny—the same people who would work comfortably with fifteen tigers go crazy when I walk in with 300,000 bees."

The bee shoot had also been dreaded because of a consensus among the filmmakers that it simply wouldn't work. "We went into the shoot believing that it was going to be a disaster," admitted Mat Beck, who fully expected to be assigned the job of generating digital bees for the dome scene. "We thought the bees would all fly up to the light. We thought we'd have trouble getting them to swarm. The attitude was, 'We'll give this a try, but it's probably going to be a bust.' But we were totally wrong. Dr. Gary and his bees were wonderful. The guys at Blue

opposite: David Duchovny awaits a shot setup on the extèrior spaceship set, built on Stage 15 at Fox. **top:** Mulder and Scully climb up through a hole in the ice to momentary safety. **bottom:** On stage, the ice field was built on a platform and covered with real snow and ice. Steam geysers were rigged from below by Paul Lombardi's special effects crew.

Sky/VIFX were still going to be generating huge swarms of computer bees of all sizes but the real ones look plenty scary."

As the second unit finished up on the bee interior, Bowman and his first-unit crew filmed scenes in and around Mulder's apartment. The small apartment and outside hallway on Stage 11—the stage that doubled as the crew's mess hall—was built to replicate the set established on the television show. "We kept the basic floor plan," said Chris Nowak, "and the basic feel of the apartment. But we tried to bring it into the feature world by making it a bit bigger and more detailed. There were certain adjustments we had to make for the big screen, without compromising the established look of the place." Filmed there was the scene in which Scully comes to Mulder's apartment to tell him she is resigning from the FBI; and in the outside hallway, the momentous occasion of a first kiss almost shared by Mulder and Scully was captured on film.

Thursday, August 14, principal photography began on Stage 15, on a set that was dubbed the exterior spaceship. But, built on a long, flat platform and covered with a layer of chipped ice, the "spaceship exterior" looked only like a blanket of snow, surrounded with green screens and giant blowups of still photographs taken at the glacier north of Vancouver. "On the exterior spaceship set," explained Chris Nowak, "we had to match the glacier that was shot at the beginning of production. We didn't have the time to go back to that location with the actors, because of their tight schedules, so we had to make an ice field on stage: a huge, open field of ice that matched what they had shot, and that had the feeling of outdoors in daylight." A layer of fake snow sufficed for the background areas of the set; but for areas closer to the action, real chipped ice was generated by ice machines and fired onto the platform between takes. "We created a twenty-five-by-

top, left: A green screen was positioned at the end of the exterior spaceship set so that imagery from the location glacier could be composited into the background for long shots. **center, left:** A special rig was devised to show Mulder and Scully rising on a section of the spaceship. **bottom, left:** Duchovny and Anderson spent several days running the length of the icy set, being hit by plumes of steam and ice fired from off-camera hoses.

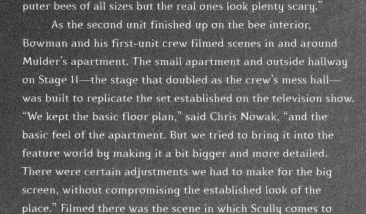

...the consistency of shaved ice, four inches deep, all spread out on a deck that was eight feet high."

The rollers, continuously hard at work to produce the fresh powder... also emanated smelly exhaust. In fact, when cast and crew members complained of headaches the first day on the set, medic Todd Adelman—concerned that the ventilation on the stage was insufficient—brought in a carbon monoxide detector the following day and discovered that the CO level first thing in the morning was 188 parts per million. "Two hundred parts per million is the beginning level of lethal," Adelman commented. "We immediately revised the ventilation system; and after that, the carbon monoxide levels were always closely monitored. They never rose above forty parts per million."

The visual simplicity of the set was misleading, for it was one of the most complicated setups of the shoot, requiring a trough and pump system to clear the area under the platform of water that collected as the ice melted, as well as steam generators to simulate geysers of ice and snow that shoot into the air as the subterranean ship begins to rise—all of which were rigged by Paul Lombardi's crew. "The whole set was built on a platform so that we could get underneath it with steam generators and air movers to create these geysers up above," explained Lombardi.

The set also created a situation in which the needs of the production designer and the needs of the director of photography—two department heads that typically work in close concert throughout film production—were at cross purposes. Chris Nowak required that the stage be refrigerated to maintain the real-ice set dressing and keep it from melting too quickly. But Ward Russell, faced with simulating bright sunlight so that the stage footage would match the glacier location footage, intended to blast the set with heat-producing lights. "That set was a tremendous challenge for me," said Russell. "Essentially, I had to recreate daylight over a 150-foot soundstage. It took a lot of lighting units to make that happen." The problem was eventually solved by an air-conditioning company that calculated the degree to which the burning lights would warm the stage, and how much refrigeration power would be necessary to override the heat of the lamps and keep the stage sufficiently cold. With multiple refrigeration units pumping cold air into the stage, the temperatures—even with the complement of bright lights burning—hovered between forty-five and fifty degrees.

On the morning of the first day of filming, the set was flanked at one end by a huge translight—a blown-up still photographed at the glacier location—that was intended to serve

below: Mulder supports Scully as they try to flee to a safe distance from the emerging ship. **below, right:** Rob Bowman and Gillian Anderson on the set while the scenes within the alien ship are being prepped.

as an in-camera background so that a visual effects background would not have to be matted into the live-action. Within hours, however, the translight was replaced by a giant green screen, and background composites were added to the visual effects slate. Visual effects producer Kurt Williams—who, with Mat Beck, had suspected that the translight would not suffice—had the green screen ready to go, and orchestrated its rigging from the stage ceiling on very short notice. "The translight was worth a try," Beck commented, "because if they'd been able to get that background in-camera, it would have saved the production a lot of time and money. But that situation was really pushing the boundaries of what a translight can do. Translights are best used for distant night backgrounds, preferably through a window, and when the focus of the action is someplace else. In this case, the translight had to blend right in with a real daylight set, *and* it was dominating the frame. Everyone quickly realized that we needed the green screen, so we could composite real backgrounds in later—and the visual effects count went up the moment the green screen did."

The live action captured on the spaceship exterior consisted primarily of Mulder and Scully running the expanse of the platform, dodging plumes of ice that rose as air movers stationed under the deck were deployed by the special effects crew. Other shots had Scully lying face down in the snow as Mulder watches the spaceship rise up before him. After multiple takes, Gillian Anderson's face went numb from the long and repeated exposure to the ice.

When first unit left the set the following week, Mat Beck stayed behind an extra day to shoot additional high-angle crane shots of stunt doubles running across the ice—footage that would be composited with visual effects shots of the glacier imploding as the rising spaceship blasts through the icy surface.

FRIDAY, AUGUST 22: ICE BUBBLE

Principal photography has moved to Stage 16, where the interior spaceship set is still in place for the rescheduled cryopod and creature shoot that will continue for the next several weeks. One corner of the stage, however, has been given over to the "ice bubble" set, erected for shots of Mulder's entrance into the ship's ventilation system, as well as his subsequent exit with Scully. "What we're filming today is Mulder's original entrance from above," says Ward Russell. "He falls through the ice floe into this cavern, going through several layers of ice until he hits the bottom. What we're doing right now is a reverse angle up at the hole from inside the bubble. Mulder sees that it is so high up, there is no way for him to climb back up and get out. So he goes down through a vent opening; and he soon discovers that it is actually a steam duct that leads to the interior of the spaceship."

As lights are set, Rob Bowman sits in his director's chair, clearly in the grips of a miserable cold. Little beads of sweat form on his nose and forehead, and he looks flushed from fever. Delicacy has been abandoned, and he clutches a huge rag that is serving as an industrial-sized handkerchief into which he blows his running nose.

opposite: The movie's climax takes place within the cavernous interior of a spaceship, settled beneath the ice in Antarctica. With information and an antidote given to him by the Well-Manicured Man, Mulder goes in search of his infected partner, who is being maintained within one of thousands of cryogenic units, used to control the gestation of the alien virus.

It is a bad day to be ill. Bowman has to cover many ice bubble shots this morning, while the afternoon will be devoted to attempting—for the second time—Mulder's rescue of Scully from the cryopod. This was the gag that went so poorly the first time around, two weeks ago. Time to film the scene is running out, as Duchovny and Anderson leave for Vancouver in only three days. Despite the pressure and his raging head cold, Bowman is as good-spirited as always. "I just feel like I'm on drugs," he jokes. "High fever has heightened my senses completely."

As Bowman plows through his slate of ice bubble shots on one side of the stage, Paul Lombardi and his crew are feverishly at work on the cryopods at the opposite end. "We got this problem dumped in our laps about two weeks ago," Lombardi says, as he brushes a coating of clear acrylic onto the front of a cryopod. "They've got to be ready to go this afternoon." Quickly moving on to the next cryopod, Lombardi pushes his silver hair out of his eyes. "This has been a real busy show for us. I said at the beginning that this was a sleeper show: one that doesn't look like it is going to have that much at the beginning, and then turns out to be really busy. And that's just what happened."

It is now nearing two o'clock in the afternoon. Gillian Anderson has been on the lot since ten, but she has not yet gone before the cameras. She has spent the day enjoying a visit from her family, escorting them, via golf cart, around the sets and into the offices of Ten Thirteen Productions, where they are greeted warmly by Chris Carter and other staff members. Anderson's two-year-old daughter, Piper, seems particularly glad to see "Uncle Chris"—although it is not clear whether it is the producer's company she treasures or the snack room next to his office that is stocked with jar after jar of candy.

Later, Anderson walks her family through the set on Stage 16, pointing out the remarkably lifelike Scully dummy that has been brought to the set by KNB, in preparation for the filming of Scully's rescue from the cryopod. As Piper eyes the dummy suspiciously, Anderson smiles and says, "That's Mommy. Mommy looks funny, huh?" Piper nods her head in agreement.

By three o'clock, Anderson has said good-bye to her family, and Piper has settled in for a nap in the actress's trailer. Anderson has still not been called before the cameras. "There are always long gaps in the day," Anderson notes, "mostly due to technical complications. But it gives me a chance to relax, to spend time with my daughter, and to get other things done. Overall, this hasn't been that exhausting an experience for me, partly because I've had more time off than David has. And even though it has been a hectic schedule, both David and I are sheltered a great deal from the stresses of making the movie. It is much harder for Dan and Chris and Lata and Rob. Their level of stress is a hundredfold what ours is."

With only three days left on the movie, Anderson is beginning to put the experience into perspective. "There have been a few really fun days," she observes, "but it has been a pretty serious shoot, primarily because of the stress the producers are experiencing. There is a lot more joking around on the set of the series than there has been here. On the show, we know that we can get the work done and still goof around to relieve the stress. But on the movie, we haven't necessarily known that we could do both at the same time. Maybe now that it's almost over, we're just starting to figure that out."

With only a few days remaining until the departure of David Duchovny and Gillian Anderson, the first-unit crew concentrated on shots of Mulder and Scully exiting the spaceship, emerging out onto the field of ice, as well as Mulder's original entrance into the ship's ventilation system from a hole in the icy surface. Both the entrance and exit scenes were shot on the "ice bubble" set, a relatively small setup representing the hole in the ice and the first few feet of the ventilation duct, built in a corner of Stage 16. As Anderson and Duchovny emerged from the duct and out onto the ice bubble, crew members threw snowballs near the actors' heads to simulate the havoc being wreaked on the snow plain. Buckets of cold water were also poured on them periodically to make the characters look suitably cold and wet.

Live-action elements of Scully's rescue from the cryopod—shots that would follow the still-unfilmed scene in which Mulder initially breaks through the pod's ice layer—were also captured in the actors' last few days of filming, including a shot of Mulder pulling the life-support tube out of Scully's mouth. "There was a long rubber string that was attached to the mouthpiece of the tube," Gillian Anderson explained, "and they wanted it to look as if this string was being pulled up from my intestines and through my throat when Mulder removed the mouthpiece. So I wrapped the string around and around my tongue; and when David pulled on the tube, I fed the string through my teeth to regulate how fast it came out of my mouth. I think it worked, and it was a lot better than having them thread this thing down my throat."

Mulder's entrance into the ice bubble was filmed the first half of the day on Friday, August 22, with the afternoon devoted to reattempting breakaway cryopod shots, both for Scully's rescue and the hatching alien sequence. All through that morning, Paul Lombardi's special effects team worked fast and furiously, putting final touches on the reconfigured cryopods and readying them for the afternoon shoot. But even with the much-improved units at their disposal, the

full spread: concept sketch of alien ship breaking out of the ice.

filmmakers continued to face major obstacles in shooting the cryopod sequences primarily because it was extremely difficult to simulate the properties of ice. "It was something no one had done before," noted art director Marc Fisichella, "so no one could come at the problem with the benefit of hindsight. We actually considered just going ahead and using real ice at one point, but that would have been very difficult. We would have needed a tremendous volume of ice in very specific configurations. And we would have had to shoot it in a very cold environment so the ice would stay frozen; and *then* we would have needed it to melt properly at just the right time. It would have been impossible." In the end, the ice effect was simulated using a variety of materials, such as resins, clear acrylics, latex, fiberglass, and—sparingly—real ice. "There wasn't one material that could do everything the sequence called for. Some materials would break away nicely, but they weren't transparent enough. Others were transparent and looked just like ice, but they didn't break easily enough. Others would break through all right, but they wouldn't crack and shatter the way ice does. Even at the very end, we were still in search of that perfect material to simulate ice—if such a thing even exists."

As the sequence was finally cut together, Scully's rescue from the cryopod starts with Mulder breaking through a sheet of real ice with the oxygen bottle he finds in the spaceship corridor. "Then it cuts to him breaking through a breakaway material on the exterior of the pod, with water and slush coming out," said David Womark. "Then, once he has actually broken through, we cut to Gillian standing in the cryopod, with real and simulated slush all around her."

Shots of creatures hatching out of the pods were also reattempted, most of them relegated to a second unit that worked on the difficult, complex series of shots throughout the last few weeks of

production and beyond. Like Scully's rescue, the hatching sequence ultimately was pieced together in painstaking cuts. "In our tests," recalled Woodruff, "we'd revealed the entire alien body breaking out of the cryopod. But by the time we got to filming the sequence, Rob and Dan and Chris had decided that they wanted to keep the creature more secretive. So the breakout from the cryopod was done primarily with isolated shots of the creature's hands breaking free. The ice covering of the pod was reinforced in certain areas so that the creature's head wouldn't break free right away, only his fists. And then, eventually, the creature butts the ice—shot with a breakaway version of the pod—and breaks through with his head."

With Bowman wrapped up in his first-unit chores, Dan Sackheim played a pivotal role in overseeing the second-unit cryopod filming, directed by Alexander Witt. "Dan had a great

deal to do with the success of the second-unit stuff inside the spaceship," Bowman commented. "He knew the storyboards intimately; and, by that time, he had come to know my tastes and what I wanted. All of the second-unit directors—not only Alexander, but also Billy Burton, who shot some of the cornfield footage, and Brian Spizer, who shot both interior and exterior spaceship footage—were excellent. But I have to give a nod to Danny for being there and championing the cause of the interior spaceship sequence."

Monday, August 25, marked the end of principal photography for David Duchovny and Gillian Anderson. Working a long, sixteen-hour day, Bowman, the actors, and the crew completed

above: Artist renderings of Mulder searching the spaceship corridor and Scully's breakout from a cryopod. **opposite:** The breakout effect proved to be one of the most difficult and time-consuming gags of the film.

the last of the actors' shots on the spaceship interior set: those of Mulder placing Scully's comatose body inside a tube, and climbing to safety as the alien hatches from a nearby cryopod. "I had four days in between the end of filming the movie and the start of filming the TV show," David Duchovny recalled. "But I couldn't complain. We all knew what we were getting ourselves into when we started this movie. It was hard, but I expected it to be hard. The worst part was working six-day weeks. That was very tough, because you feel as if you have no down time at all. I don't ever want to work six-day weeks again." A handful of shots and scenes—such as the crucial scene between Mulder and the Cigarette-Smoking Man at movie's end—remained unfilmed, and would have to be picked up sometime in the following months, worked around the actors' television production schedules.

With the departure of Anderson and Duchovny, the most pressing phase of the production schedule had ended, but any sense of relief was momentary, at best. "If I felt a lessening of the pressure at all," recalled Rob Bowman, "it lasted for all of a minute. Because, at that point, we went immediately into some of the very hard sequences that we'd put off to the end of the schedule. We sent Gillian and David off on the plane, wished them well, and then stared ahead at the mountain of work that was left behind."

Most of that mountain of work was situated on Stage 14, where the art and construction departments had created a large cave set. "The design of the cave set went through six or seven incarnations," recalled Dan Sackheim. "Some of the changes were conceptual in nature, but most were due to our trying to find a way to build the set within a certain budget. Chris Nowak had to keep reconfiguring it because there just wasn't enough time or money to build it as it was initially conceived."

Those initial concepts had called for three separate sets: one to represent the ice cave featured in the film's open-

ing sequence; one modern-day cave for Stevie's fall and rescue; and another for Dr. Bronschweig's ice cave, dressed with high-tech monitoring equipment, walkways, lights, and isolation tents. But, faced with the limitations of the budget, Nowak—as he had done for the spaceship interior—configured a singular set that would serve as all three cave settings. "It was an interesting logistical puzzle," Nowak noted, "figuring out how to make all of those changes in the time we had available. We

opposite: After discovering Scully within one of the spaceship cryopods, Mulder breaks through the thick icy covering and injects her with the life-saving antidote. **below:** This shot of Scully with her mouth wide open does not appear anywhere in the movie; it was shot strictly to give the special effects team a base image with which to work when developing the icy tube.

worked with Josh McLaglen, the first assistant director, to figure out the best sequence of shooting, so that we could start
with the most complicated version of the cave, and then go on
to the less complicated versions, because it is always easier to
take things out than to put things in." The devised schedule
called for filming to begin with the primitive ice cave—the most
complex version of the set—and then move on to Stevie's cave,
and finally, Dr. Bronschweig's testing facility.

Constructed by Billy Iiams and his crew, the cave set was
framed in lumber, covered with wire mesh and plaster that was
carved to give it a rocklike texture, then painted to match the
coloration of the California City location that had served as the
cave's topside. To transform the desert cave into its primitive,
icy counterpart, carved fiberglass walls, treated to simulate ice,
were flown into the set. Chipped ice—manufactured outside the
stage, and wheelbarrowed in by crew members—was also
spread around specific shooting areas. Like the exterior spaceship set, the ice cave was refrigerated to keep the snow from
melting too quickly under the hot lights. The dark, moody
atmosphere of the ice cave scenes required much less illumina-
tion, however, and thus, fewer heat-producing lighting instruments; and so the refrigerated stage remained ten to fifteen
degrees colder than the temperatures on the exterior spaceship
set, dipping to between twenty-eight and thirty-two degrees.

Among the scenes captured in the week-long ice cave
shoot were the primitives' hunt for the alien and the attack that
ends with the creature's death. Featuring many appearances by
the creature, the shoot was a busy one for Tom Woodruff, outfit-
ted in the foam latex suit that was covered in slime to give it a
photogenic sheen. "We had intended to leave the primitive alien
dry, without slime, because we thought it would make him look
older," said Woodruff. "But we found that it just didn't look as
good without it. Once we slimed the suit up with methocel—the
gel we usually use—the colors became more vibrant and more
real. The creature's skin didn't look like rubber anymore."

Blind inside the creature head, Woodruff found it particularly difficult to perform the complex and high-energy action
scenes on the icy, slippery cave set. After several hours of working without benefit of sight, Woodruff finally removed one of
the creature's black eyes to provide a window through which he
could see. "We were shooting this scene in such low light,"
Woodruff said, "you couldn't tell that an eye was missing. It just
looked like a black hole, which is what the eyes looked like anyway. So we took it out. My vision was still obstructed, but I
could see enough to get by."

TUESDAY, AUGUST 26: ICE CAVE

With the departure of Gillian Anderson and David Duchovny, the production has now turned to the filming of scenes that do not feature Mulder and Scully. Today marks the first day within the ice cave set on Stage 14, which, like the exterior spaceship set, has been refrigerated to maintain the man-made snow covering the stage.

On the set today are Lance Anderson and his prosthetic makeup crew, who arrived before six A.M. to apply makeups to Craig Davis and Carrick O'Quinn, the actors portraying the primitive men featured in the movie's opening sequence. This is the makeup artists' first day of work on the film since June, when they traveled to the glacier in Canada to apply the primitive makeups for the second-unit shoot there. The only work required in the interim was a slight change in one of the makeups. "They wanted a slightly more narrow jaw on one of the characters," Anderson explains. "The wider jaw was all right for what they shot up on the glacier, because those were all long

shots anyway. But once we got back from Canada, ADI started making the new jaw pieces so that they would be ready for these five days of filming on the set."

Application of the entire prosthetic makeup—including body makeup and dirt and grime applied to exposed areas of the skin—took three and a half hours, initially; but with practice, the application time has been shortened to two and a half hours. "It's going very smoothly," Anderson says as he steps outside the freezing stage to enjoy the warmth of the sun. "It is so cold on that set, at least we don't have to worry about the makeup sweating off the actors. Usually, we have a lot of trouble making the appliance pieces stick, because of all the sweating and heat under the lights. But we may have to chisel it off at the end of the day today, because the makeups have frozen to the actors' faces. It's thirty-two degrees in there!"

Entering from the bright sunlight outside the stage, the set is especially dark, lit mainly by a torch carried by one of the primitives as he makes his way down a narrow icy corridor, in search of the creature. The character's point of view through the forty-foot-long tunnel is filmed by a Steadicam operator who follows directly behind the actor, capturing only the primitive's hand holding the burning torch in the foreground.

After a few takes, Bowman is still not satisfied with the movement of the torch in the shot. Finally, he has some appropriately grimy makeup applied to his own hand by Lance Anderson. Then he takes up the torch himself and makes his way through the tunnel, stooping low and waving the flaming torch as the Steadicam operator follows closely behind him.

Mat Beck was also on hand for the ice cave shoot, specifically for the filming of the scene in which the dead creature's black, oily blood crawls up the primitive's body. "The blood of the alien is an organism in and of itself," said Beck. "We see it move purposefully onto the primitive's chest, neck, and face. We'd had to come up with the same kind of effect for episodes of the TV show, and we'd used all kinds of tricks to make that happen." While practical methods for creating the effect had been devised for the television show, the black "worms" sequence in the movie would be computer generated, then composited into live-action plates. To facilitate the process of combining CG and live-action elements, the on-set primitive was filmed by a camera mounted to a motion control system, which provided smooth and repeatable camera movement. "With the motion control system," said Beck, "we didn't get any of the unexpected, herky-jerky movements you sometimes get when you have to rely on a human camera operator. It gave us a smooth, predictable, upward movement on the primitive, which would make the tracking of the CG worm elements that much easier. It also meant we could shoot the cave wall in a separate pass, with more visual effects-friendly lighting."

Tracking is the means by which an element that was not actually filmed on the set, such as the CG blood, is married to the live action. In the case of the ice cave scene, the CG blood would be attached to a CG representation of the primitive, which, in turn, would be tracked to align perfectly with the real actor in the scene. In addition, virtual camera movements on

the CG blood and CG primi-
tive would have to correspond exactly
with the movements of the camera in the original
plate. In earlier days of CG effects, tracking required that
extensive measurements and data be gathered on the live-
action set. As the technology developed, high-tech devices
such as laser surveying systems aimed at targets provided
the tracking data. In general, any stationary, solid object in
the scene could serve as a target, and visual effects teams
would often place such objects in the set during the filming
of their plates, then remove them from the footage digitally
once their tracking chores were accomplished.

The ice cave primitive scenes were so dark, however, no
such targets could have been detected. "The problem was that
we were tracking to a moving, emoting human face," Beck
explained. "And it was too dark in the torchlight to lock on to
landmarks like the bridge of his nose. So, I put little tracking
dots, made out of front projection material, all over the primitive, so that I could see them clearly in a faint light from the
camera. Then, instead of shooting the primitive at the normal
rate of twenty-four frames per second, we shot him at forty-

eight
frames
per second.
Mounted to the
lens of the camera was
a ring of LED lights that flashed
every other frame. Filming at forty-eight frames
per second, with the camera flashing every other frame,
we got twenty-four frames every second that had these
tracking dots on the primitive; and we got another twenty-four
frames every second in which the dots didn't show up at all,
since the tracking dots were revealed only when the LED lights
flashed. So we had tracking marks to use every other frame, and

above: The primitive finds something shocking frozen in the ice of the cave.

a clean image
every other frame, which
meant we didn't have to go in
and remove those tracking dots
after the fact."

Another challenging aspect of the ice
cave scene, from a visual effects standpoint, was
that the primitive was clothed in dark fur, which
obscured the black organisms as they moved over him.
"His black fur clothing would have made it virtually impossible to see the blood," said Beck. "Fortunately, we were able to
turn the skin he was wearing inside out where the blood
would be, so at least it was suede there, instead of fur."

Following the ice cave shoot—and a three-day Labor
Day weekend—the set on Stage 14 was cleared of the fiberglass
ice walls and snow, then rearranged into its modern-day

configuration for the filming of Stevie's fall and
the subsequent rescue sequence. A blue screen was hung over
the top of the set so that the stage ceiling could be replaced by
a real sky shot in California City.

Shots of the oily substance moving into Stevie's shoe,
unlike the primitive worms sequence, were lit brightly enough
to allow for traditional tracking methods, without the support
of the LED light rig.

Illuminated dots were applied to actor Lucas Black to aid
the postproduction tracking. "I told him that these dots wouldn't
leave *too* much of a rash," Mat Beck joked, "and that it would
clear up by the time he was nineteen or twenty."

Black—introduced to movie-going audiences through his
pivotal role in *Slingblade*—was on set for only a couple of
days, as production captured Stevie's terrifying, and ultimately fatal experience within the cave. "Lucas was just wonderful," Tricia Ronten recalled. "He brought so much life to

the character of Stevie. We were all sad that he had so few days with us. He is an amazingly brilliant kid, and a wonderful actor. He had to do this whole scene, reacting to something that wasn't there—the black worms—and he did it beautifully. In fact, he got all the way through it, and his performance had gone really well; and then we realized that the motion control camera had moved backward. So he had to do it all over again. It was very late in the day, and he was so tired. It was a tough thing for a kid. But he did the whole scene over again, and he was brilliant."

V THE SHOOT: LOCATIONS REVISITED

Location filming picked up on Wednesday, September 3, when the production moved to the Atheneum Club at the California Institute of Technology in Pasadena to shoot the first day of a long scene between the Syndicate elders in a Kensington men's club. The following days in Pasadena found the company at the "Batman House"—the exterior location used to represent Wayne Manor in the *Batman* television series. Scenes filmed there included the Well-Manicured Man watching his grandchildren playing outside his elegant London estate, as well as an interior shot of him taking the call that summons him to the elders meeting.

On Monday, September 8, the production returned to Bakersfield to shoot another cornfield for the movie's final

above: On the set for the London office where we see the Syndicate meet.

scene, set in a Tunisian landscape, dotted with bee domes. "We used a cornfield that was very near to the one we shot before," said David Womark. "But in this case, it is supposed to be out in the middle of the Sahara Desert, where news about the fate of the conspiracy arrives."

"The movie ends with the sense that Mulder hasn't really stopped anything," elaborated Rob Bowman. "We see the cornfield and bee domes in Tunisia, and we know that the Project is still going. And there is the final scene between the Cigarette-Smoking Man and Conrad Strughold, in which the Cigarette-Smoking Man notes that Mulder has turned out to be a very worthy, sturdy opponent. Strughold tries to shrug it off, saying, 'What can one man do?' But the performance is played in such a way that his expression belies his words. He knows that Mulder is a formidable enemy."

Another revisited location was California City, where production continued on Tuesday and Wednesday, September 9 and 10, shooting exteriors of Bronschweig's camp. "It wasn't the easiest way to shoot a movie," Womark admitted, "going to a location with the lead actors, then returning weeks later to do the other stuff. But it was the only way we could work out the logistics of the schedule. So we had to do this whirlwind tour at the end of the schedule, going back to some of those locations to pick up what we didn't have time to get before."

Thursday, September 11, the first unit ended its location tour, returning to Stage 14 at the Fox lot to shoot its last set: the interiors of Bronschweig's cave. The cave set had been reconfigured one more time by the art department and construction crews, with cave walls being repositioned—a major task in itself, due to the weight of the plaster set pieces—and set dressings

such as monitors, refrigeration units, and a containment tent added to the basic cave setting. "The containment tent was a kind of makeshift cryopod," explained Marc Fisichella, "in which the body of the fireman is maintained at a low temperature so that the embryo can gestate to full term."

Because the crew had traveled back from California City the night before, the call for the first day of the Bronschweig's cave shoot was not until one o'clock in the afternoon. The day was devoted primarily to establishing the cave interior. "We shot

opposite, top: A mansion in Pasadena also served as the estate of the Well-Manicured Man, seen watching his grandchildren at play. opposite, bottom: John Neville as the Well-Manicured Man, Armin Mueller-Stahl as Conrad Strughold, and William B. Davis as the Cigarette-Smoking Man, on the Pasadena set of the London Syndicate office. above: Mulder and Scully con their way into the morgue at Bethesda Naval Hospital.

Bronschweig walking through the cave," Fisichella commented, "which allowed us to establish the whole setup. Later that night, we shot the scene where Bronschweig returns to the area and finds that the alien has hatched from the fireman's body." While filming of the scenes went smoothly, the day took a downward spin when David Womark slipped on the slick paraffin surface around the containment unit and hit his head against the hard plaster set. After receiving medical care at a local hospital, where he received several stitches, Womark returned to the set and worked until the company wrapped for the day.

While the first unit focused on the Bronschweig cave scenes, E. J. Forester's second unit was back on the Pemberton Ice Cap, filming the entrance to a real ice cave for the opening sequence—footage that would tie in with ice cave interiors

filed on this same stage at the end of August. "We couldn't shoot it when we were up there at the beginning of the schedule," explained Womark, "because the ice doesn't melt enough to open up those caves until August or September. So at the end of the schedule, we had a Vancouver unit go back up to the glacier to shoot the introduction of the ice cave sequence."

During the same period, Dan Sackheim took a forty-person crew to London for filming of exteriors of the men's club where the syndicate elders meet, the interiors of which had been filmed in Pasadena the previous week. With a huge volume of primitive and creature material still to shoot, and realizing that he could not afford to take five days away from the stages to shoot a mere five exteriors in London, Bowman decided to remain in Los Angeles and turn the shots over to Sackheim. "Danny probably did a better job of shooting the London exteriors than I would have done anyway," Bowman commented, "because, at that point in the schedule, I was pretty much toast. He also added some shots that were great, expanding the scene into something better than what I'd had in mind. He shot all of my storyboards, but because he was there with a fresh mind, he was able to add to them."

Sackheim and his crew were in London for a week, with several days devoted to prep before a single day of filming. "We shot near Albert Hall," recalled Sackheim. "It was a big deal to go all the way to London for half a page of script; but it was worth it because we got a lot of production value. It gave the movie a greater sense of verisimilitude and greater scope. We wanted to show all of that London atmosphere in the movie, the double-decker buses and all of that."

The final days of the principal photography schedule were spent shooting three major makeup and creature effects scenes: the alien attack on Bronschweig, which required not only

top: On the Syndicate office set, Rob Bowman confers with Armin Mueller-Stahl prior to shooting the long, dialogue-heavy scene. **bottom:** A crucial scene between the Cigarette-Smoking Man and Strughold at film's end, set in Tunisia, reveals that the clandestine project has not been stopped.

Woodruff's performance in the alien suit, but also a prosthetic makeup on actor Jeffrey DeMunn; shots of the cave fireman, which would employ the articulated, transparent fireman body with the alien embryo inside; and shots featuring the fireman after the alien has burst from his body.

The mauled-Bronschweig makeup had been designed and fabricated by ADI more than a month prior to its filming. "It was an extensive makeup," noted Alec Gillis, "because Bronschweig is really torn apart by the alien. Chris and Rob wanted to go far with that makeup, because

the television show. They can't get too gory, because they have to worry about ratings. This was their opportunity to really show some gruesome stuff. We generally stay away from really gory effects; but in this case, it was essential to the story."

Because DeMunn lived on the East Coast and would not be in the Southern California area until it was time for him to report to the *X-Files* movie set, Gillis and Woodruff commissioned New York–based makeup effects artist John Dods to take a lifecast of the actor. "We needed to get started on it right away," said Woodruff, "so we had John cast the actor back there." The makeup was designed by sculpting over the casting of the actor's head. "The goal was to come up with a makeup effect that was gruesome, but not so gruesome that it would be cut from the movie. We had to show that this guy was under a vicious attack. It had to be something that would counteract any perception that these aliens were full of wisdom and caring. This had to make the audience and the characters in the movie think, 'Oh shit, what do we do now?' Technically, it wasn't that

actually happening on screen. It was more a matter of showing alien claws coming at Bronschweig in a few shots; and then, later, revealing him in this mauled makeup. We wound up putting several appliance pieces on him, hiding tubes that we could pump blood through."

ADI also provided the cave fireman understudy by Bronschweig, which was designed to suggest a relatively early stage of alien infestation. "At that stage," explained Woodruff, "the fireman's skin has gone clear and there is a living creature embryo inside of him, moving around. You can see its eyes blinking inside the fireman's body. So, we had to create an effect within an effect: an articulated alien embryo within an articulated fireman body. The fireman body was transparent, so you could see some bone structure and some remnants of tissue and muscle underneath in the arms and legs; but all you could really see inside the torso was the alien puppet moving around."

The first step, as always, was to do a lifecast of the actor portraying the afflicted fireman—in this case, casting him from

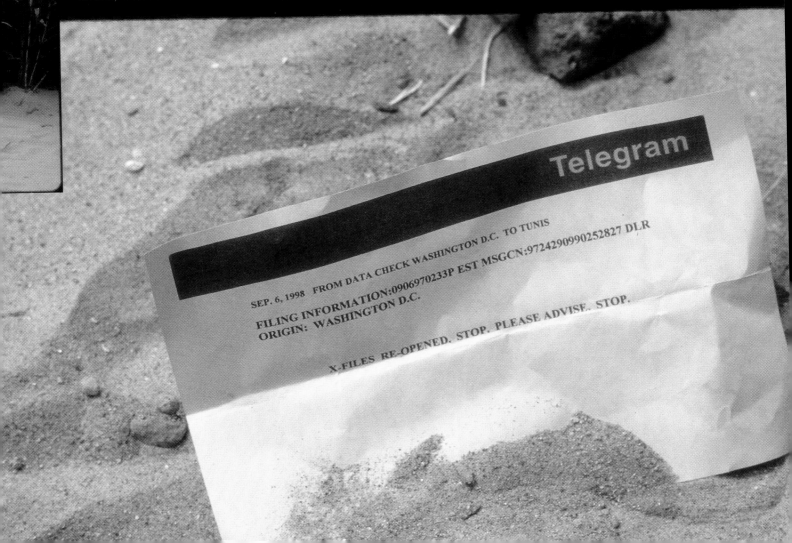

Telegram

SEP. 6, 1998 FROM DATA CHECK WASHINGTON D.C. TO TUNIS

FILING INFORMATION:0906970233P EST MSGCN:9724290990252827 DLR

ORIGIN: WASHINGTON D.C.

X-FILES RE-OPENED. STOP. PLEASE ADVISE. STOP.

body had to be created. That lifecast was then duplicated in clay to enable the ADI artists to resculpt, making the body appear distended in the torso area, where the alien would be, and more withered in the limbs. Molds were then taken from that sculpture and used to run pieces of a specially formulated silicone material. "There have been some great silicones developed over the past few years," noted Woodruff. "We can make them clear, yet very soft and flexible, like flesh. We were able to control those qualities in the molds, building up the thickness that we wanted. The thicker it is, the less clear it is, so we had to be careful about that. But we wanted a certain amount of translucence, because it wouldn't have looked organic if it had been completely clear. It would have looked like an ice sculpture. We did some tests early on to determine the best thickness of skin that would be clear enough to allow us to see some of the form underneath, yet translucent enough to look real and show detail of form."

Tests were also conducted to develop a technique for adding veins and muscle tissue to the body interior. "In our tests," said Woodruff, "we actually let a layer of silicone set, then painted veins and muscle tissue on that; set another layer, and painted that, and so on, creating a real sense of depth in the vein networks. But when we got to actually building the bodies, we changed to a simpler technique. We built a core that represented the internal structure of the body—a little bit of bone and muscle—and we painted veins right on that core. So the bones and the muscle and all of that stuff you see inside the fireman is really just a one-piece sculpture. The clear silicone skin went over that, and was painted with an additional surface coating of veins." Final stages of building the fireman body included putting in acrylic eyes and teeth, then punching real human hair into the head and body, one hair at a time. "That made it dead-on real looking, as if the hair was actually growing out of this translucent skin."

For the alien embryo inside the fireman's body, ADI created a sculpture, from which the final foam latex creature was made. Like the full-size aliens, the embryo had an articulated head, operated via radio control. "He was capable of blinking and opening his jaw," said Woodruff. "Then, for more general body movement, we put little rods coming out from his backside, so puppeteers could get back there and move him around a little bit. He was sculpted in a fetal position; but he was able to move his shoulders and scootch around as if he was trying to make himself comfortable." A window cut into the core in the back of the fireman body gave puppeteers access to the puppet rods. "Everybody was thrilled with the embryo and the cave fireman when we got to shooting it. The fireman was lying there with his eyes open, his head rolling around, and his jaw opening as if he was taking his last breath. Inside his chest, you could see his lungs expanding and his heart pumping and a vein throbbing in his neck as the embryo brought its face up to the transparent skin of the torso. The embryo blinked and moved its hands and jaws. It was very effective. Out of everything we did on the show, that was the effect that elicited the most startled response from everybody on the set. They were amazed."

A second, nonarticulated version of the fireman was constructed for the scene in which Bronschweig discovers that the alien has "hatched" from the dead man's body. Built similarly to the earlier version, the limbs were more withered and there appeared to be even less organic material remaining inside the man—both to suggest a more progressed stage of infection. The

torso area was also sculpted to look as if it had been ripped open by the emerging alien.

Principal photography on the *X-Files* movie wrapped on Tuesday, September 16, but there was little sense of real completion, as there were still many shots on the second-unit agenda. Freed from his first-unit duties, Rob Bowman directed much of the remaining second-unit material. "The only difference for me," said Bowman, "was that there were fewer people on the set every day. But I was still shooting: more creature stuff, more cryopod inserts." The shoot was finally completed at the end of the first week in October, when

full spread: The last days of principal photography were spent on the interior cave set, reconfigured to represent Bronschweig's high-tech testing facility. The set was framed in wood, covered in sculpted plaster, and dressed with monitors, computers, and a refrigerated containment tent.

Bowman filmed the scene in which Scully's comatose body—one of the KNB props, situated within a mocked-up containment unit—is loaded onto a plane bound for the Antarctic. "It was the last day of second unit, the very last thing I shot. We shot it at LAX, at the American International cargo area, right at the end of the runway. It was an all-nighter—a big night with lots of big lights and jets going by."

he is unflappable. This guy had road blocks thrown at him time and time again, and I never once saw him lose his cool. He would have been justified in losing his cool on many, many occasions, but he always handled himself so well. His facility for adapting and making changes on the spot was remarkable. He handled whatever was thrown at him with grace and composure and a great degree of skill. I really give him credit for that."

"Directing at this level of complexity and at this pace required being in almost a Zen state," Bowman acknowledged, "which I achieved daily by going into my trailer at lunch to be alone and to refocus on the story I was trying to tell. There are so many distractions on a set, so many fires that need to be put out, that it is easy to be torn away from the purity of telling that story. So I'd go into my trailer and sit and remember the essence of what I was doing there.

"I also held on to something a friend of mine said at the

Four months had elapsed since the start of filming *The X-Files*, and every day of that four months had presented the filmmakers with challenges born of a too-short prep and an equally restricted shooting schedule. No one was more in the line of fire throughout the shoot than Rob Bowman; but, somehow, he had maintained an admirable composure from the first day of filming to the last. "One of the extraordinary things about Rob," noted Dan Sackheim, "is that

beginning: 'Navigate through the storm.' I felt as if I was in a very small boat, going through a very big storm at sea. And it seemed as if I was going to lose the ship many times. But the image of myself at the wheel of that boat, hanging on, navigating through the storm, helped me to get through a level of intensity and stress that otherwise would have made me lose my mind. There are so many reasons to blow up, every day. But I don't create very well if I allow myself to explode. I don't like working in that atmosphere. And if I'm blowing, I'm not navigating through the storm."

VI: THE POST

With the completion of filming, the movie entered a seven-month-long postproduction, an extended period that was leisurely in comparison to the frantic prep and production schedules. "The plan," said Chris Carter, "was to have a finished version of the movie, without the CG shots, by Christmas. That would give us the following several months to look at it and perfect it and add in the CG shots. It seemed like a real luxury of time, but we needed every bit of it." Released from the immediate demands of the film, Carter shifted his full-time attention to the television show, traveling to Vancouver to oversee production of episodes he had written himself. Left behind at Fox were Rob Bowman and Dan Sackheim, who would spend the next three months editing hundreds of reels of film into a cohesive, two-hour movie.

Bowman and editor Steve Mark initiated the process with the exterior spaceship sequence, the heaviest effects scene in the film. Live-action elements of the sequence had to be cut together as quickly as possible so that the visual effects team could immediately begin generating and compositing its shots. "That sequence was going to be fabricated almost entirely by effects," Bowman noted, "so I had to make a lot of guesses when it came to editing the scene. I had to imagine what would be happening, once the effects were in, and try to be optimistic about how it would all turn out. I structured the sequence to build to a nice climax, then turned it over to Mat Beck."

After devoting the first week and a half exclusively to cutting the exterior spaceship material, Bowman and Mark then began editing the film in continuity, starting with reel one, an editing approach Bowman had determined would be the most efficient. "I was very driven to get back to the television show in Vancouver," Bowman said, "so I wanted to get as much work on the movie behind me as possible. I decided that the best way to edit this movie was to go in continuity. There was a lot of film, and the story was very complex, so that seemed like the best approach." Just as Bowman had adjusted his directing style somewhat for the filming of the movie, he found that a different pace in the editing was mandated, as well. "On TV, you are always trying to hold on to your audience and keep them from changing the channel. There is more urgency to it, and more cuts. But in a feature, the audience has driven to the theater, they've paid their money, they are sitting there with their

opposite: Housed inside the containment unit is the dying, infected cave fireman.

popcorn, and they are not going to get up and walk out of there unless you've screwed it up pretty badly. You've got their interest and their attention, so you don't have to pummel them to death with changing images. A lot of filmmakers do that, very successfully, but it's not my style. I'm a bit of a throwback in my tastes, and what I really love are old, classic movies. In both shooting and editing this movie, I wasn't trying to be new or hip or a vanguard, setting new ground for filmmaking. I was trying to give it an old-fashioned, classic flavor."

Even as it was being edited, the film was incomplete. Missing were all of the visual effects, as well as pickup shots that had fallen through the cracks during the busy production schedule. Those pickups included green screen shots of Mulder and Scully for the exterior spaceship sequence, and shots of Mulder climbing through a ventilation duct as he makes his way into the interior of the ship. "We'd shot the beginning of that," noted Dan Sackheim, "when he falls through the hole in the ice; and we'd shot the end, when he emerges into the spaceship interior. But we hadn't shot the middle section, when he is actually climbing through this vent. We'd just run out of time."

Also missing was a crucial encounter between Mulder and the Cigarette-Smoking Man, intended to play near the end of the film. The scene was one of the last to be written by Carter, who intentionally avoided nailing down the exchange until he could see how the rest of the movie played out. "It was a very important scene," said Sackheim, "but we never fit it into the production schedule. We ended principal photography knowing that we'd have to pick up that scene at some point." The missing shots and scenes would be worked in around the busy television production schedules of David Duchovny and Gillian Anderson. "We just had to chip away at these shots, on weekends, or whenever we could. It was an unfortunate situation, because the actors were already up to their eyeballs in work."

In addition to editing, Bowman and Sackheim spent much of the period between the end of the shoot in October and Christmas interfacing with the visual effects department, reviewing tests, and offering their input. Bowman had assumed that his involvement in the visual effects work at this stage would be minimal—just as it had always been on the television show, where time for back-and-forth between the director and the visual effects team is virtually nonexistent. "I soon discovered that there wasn't a single detail in the effects that didn't require my input," Bowman commented. "It *all* had to be directed. I had to be there to put my signature on these shots and make sure they fit within the concept of the overall film."

While he had been on set throughout the production schedule, shooting plates, visual effects supervisor Mat Beck was only now beginning to produce shots for the show. February was the original delivery date for the visual effects; but that deadline was pushed back when the shot count, inevitably, grew. With visual effects producer Kurt Williams, Beck was responsible for providing four major effects sequences: the "worm" sequences, in which the creature's black, oily blood crawls up the bodies of one of the primitives and, later, Stevie; the explosion of the FEMA building; the digital set extensions for the interior of the spaceship; and the alien spacecraft sequence at the film's climax. In addition to those major effects sequences, the visual effects team would execute a number of composites, providing Dallas skylines and fields of corn where none had actually existed.

Beck's own visual effects company, Light Matters, took on the challenge of computer generating the images for the worm sequences,

way that made sense, based on what the character was doing. We couldn't just go off and animate them any way we wanted to. Making the stuff look real and fluid and *purposeful* was the real challenge."

The effects were ultimately created through either metaballs or surface digital techniques. "Metaballs is a subset of CG in which you have globules that are joined together," explained Beck. "With metaballs, you form your model out of these interacting globules, each of which can be animated and controlled separately. The other technique was to create a mesh surface that could be stretched and pulled in various directions simply by pulling on the control vertices that went into that surface. Then we could put a surface on that mesh and light it. Ultimately that is the way we went."

The Stevie worm sequence differed from the scene at the opening of the film in that, after crawling into the boy's shoe, the worms are revealed moving beneath his skin, rather than on the surface. "Having the worms move beneath the skin was a harder effect because it required deforming the skin," said Beck. "We had to model Stevie's body in CG, then wrap that model with the texture of his skin. We stretched his skin texture—taken from the live-action footage—over the wire-frame model, then deformed it to suggest this liquid was moving under there."

While Light Matters was developing the worms, Blue Sky/VIFX was working on the explosion of the government building early in the film. Pyrotechnics rigged into a false front on the abandoned UNOCAL

first scanning the actor portraying the primitive to create a computer model of his chest and head. The team animated and tracked computer-generated black fluid to that CG representation of the primitive, which was subsequently tracked to the real actor in the live-action footage. "Greg Strause's tracking of the CG head to the real head had to be dead-on," Beck remarked, "otherwise, the worms would have been dancing all over the place."

During his tenure as visual effects supervisor on the *X-Files* television show, Beck had created a similar effect practically, mounting the lights, cameras, and a portion of the set on a gimbal, then tilting the entire setup to make the liquid flow in the desired direction and at the appropriate speed. "You could see the liquid change direction and move in this very purposeful way," Beck recalled. "We thought about doing the same thing for the movie, but decided against it because the schedule didn't allow for what would have been a very time-consuming practical effects gag. And, since it would have worked for some shots but not for others, we would have ended up having to create some CG blood anyway. Once you know that some of the shots will have to be CG, there is little point in not doing them *all* CG."

While tests had been conducted previously, Colin Strause at Light Matters began generating the CG worms in earnest approximately one month after principal photography wrapped. Strause focused on the primitive sequence first, building a computer model for the organic, worm-like substance, then animating it to migrate up the primitive's body. To develop characteristics such as color, thickness, and viscosity, the visual effects team relied on reference footage of various moving liquids, as well as input from Chris Carter and Rob Bowman; but the animation itself had been predetermined by the primitive's performance in the live-action plate. "The animation for the worm movement was completely driven by that actor's performance," Beck commented. "In order for this scene to work, the worms had to be moving in a

opposite, left: Early drawings of the interior cave. **opposite, right:** The crew to shoot Bronschweig after his mauling by the alien. **above:** Members of Bronschweig's team realize they need to leave him behind. **right:** ADI designed the multiple-appliance mauled makeup.

building in downtown Los Angeles had provided live-action elements of the blast; and that live-action footage was augmented with three visual effects shots, achieved through model photography. Those shots were initially designed and developed through computer-generated previsualizations. "We had to figure out what the flavor of the destruction was going to be," noted Kurt Williams. "Should there be emergency lights flashing, for example, or should it look like dead, dusty concrete lying on the ground? We had to come up with ways to make the explosion aftermath come alive, with lights and broken water pipes and other details."

Crucial reference for the look of the explosion was provided by a computer-simulated analysis of the Oklahoma City bombing, which revealed an initial blast in the lower region of the structure, followed by the collapse of the building's upper levels. "We wanted our explosion to work basically the same way," said Beck, "as if the bomb situated down low knocks the pins out of the building, causing everything else to collapse, with sheets of masonry just falling away." As it plays in the final sequence, the explosion starts in tight on Mulder and Scully as they run from the building, hop in a car, and speed away. "The action is played from their point of view, so you don't really see that much of the actual explosion going off. In fact, in a real explosion, there is so much smoke and dust, it is difficult to really see what is going on anyway. It is only after the car Mulder and Scully are in crashes as a result of the concussive wave that you see what is happening with the building. So in our model photography, we had to show more of the aftermath than the actual explosion itself. And what do you see in the aftermath? You see floors collapse, you see debris flying, you see water spouting, you see little fires burning and ambient sparks and smoke. A lot had to go on with the miniature, but it didn't have to show a big fireball going up on the initial explosion itself."

Three views of the destruction were realized through model photography: a shot looking straight down from the top of the building as the walls fall away and a cloud of dust rises; a long-distance view revealing the collapse of the building's left side; and a pan past Mulder as he stands in front of the destroyed building. "It is the shot where he says to Scully, 'Next time, you buy.' There is still a little bit of debris falling, there is smoke, and you see water spraying up from broken water pipes."

An eighth-scale, twenty-three-foot-tall miniature was built by the model makers at Hunter/Gratzner Industries, under the supervision of Ian Hunter. Rather than recreate the entire building in miniature, however, Beck had opted to save time and money by commissioning a wedge-shaped model. The left side of the miniature was built in full three-dimensional depth, while the right side angled in to form the pointed end of the pie shape. "The cost would have been too high if we'd built the entire building as a model," Beck commented. "But the cheat worked because of the camera angles we'd picked. From those angles, you'd never see the entire three-dimensional structure anyway. Most of the destruction is on the left side of the building; and on the right side, there is almost no destruction at all, except for the breaking of windows. So we decided to build the depth of the building only on the left side, and film it from that side, at an angle."

Made of a steel frame covered with drywall and clear plastic windows, the miniature was lavishly detailed on the inside and out to make it look like multiple floors of offices. "There was broken rebar and ceiling tiles and all kinds of little details on it," Beck stated. "If you looked in the windows, you'd see clocks, stopped at the exact time the script says the explosion takes place. Ian Hunter even put little calendars inside, including one that had a big 'X' on Chris Carter's birthday, October 13."

The explosion of the building miniature was shot at the abandoned Hughes Aircraft facility in Playa Vista, just a few miles from the Fox lot. Previously, the facility's large, soundstage-sized hangars had served productions such as *Titanic*, *Batman Forever*, and *Independence Day*. For *The X-Files*, the model team erected the miniature in a parking lot at the facility. "It is always better to shoot an outdoor miniature outdoors, if possible," explained Beck. "We set it up and shot it in the right sunlight so that it would match the live-action lighting. It meant we had to guess what the weather was going to do. We had to consider wind, clouds, rain, all of those conditions that aren't supposed to be a problem in L.A., that are *always* a problem in L.A." Weather was more of a concern than usual, since news reports were full of dire warnings about the torrential rains that were supposed to hit Southern California, due to El Niño. In fact, predictions of heavy rains in late Fall accounted for the decision to shoot the model near the end of October, and no later.

Three days were allotted for the miniature shoot—Monday, October 27 through Wednesday, October 29—which was supervised by Beck, with John Wash and a film crew from Blue Sky/VIFX doing the actual filming, and a crew from Hunter/Gratzner on hand to see to dressing and resetting chores on the model. Miniature pyrotechnician Ian O'Connor was charged with rigging small fires throughout the model, as well as detonating plumes of debris. "In the wide shot," said Beck, "we see a big secondary collapse of the top floors, with debris falling. And then we see the collapse of the roof, which was made out of a very thin rubber material so that it would drape like a broken sail. There was a shot like that of the roof of the Oklahoma City building, and I thought it was one of the most poignant images from that explosion." Collapsible floors were supported by cylinders and specially rigged wires, released via remote control to make specific levels of the building collapse on cue.

When the miniature shoot was over, Beck and the Blue Sky/VIFX team had all of the elements necessary to produce their final three shots. The wide view of the miniature was composited with live-action footage of the real building in downtown Los Angeles, as well as with stock footage of Dallas. The down-angle from the roof was also composited into footage of the real explosion on the UNOCAL building, which included views of Mulder and Scully's car driving away. "When it was final," Beck explained, "that shot consisted of real background, the real car, some real smoke, separately shot smoke elements, and miniature elements of the facade falling down the face of the building." Finally, a small section of the destroyed miniature was composited into the green screen area around Mulder for the live-action pan.

While traditional model effects photography was executed for the building explosion, another major sequence in the movie—the interior spaceship—required a digital solution, with the set built onstage extended through a combination of 2-D and 3-D computer-generated images. Initially, the digital technicians at Light Matters had been assigned nine set extension shots; but when the sequence was finally cut together, nearly thirty such shots were required. The increase was due to the compositional limitations imposed by filming on a set that represented only a tiny fraction of what would ultimately be seen in

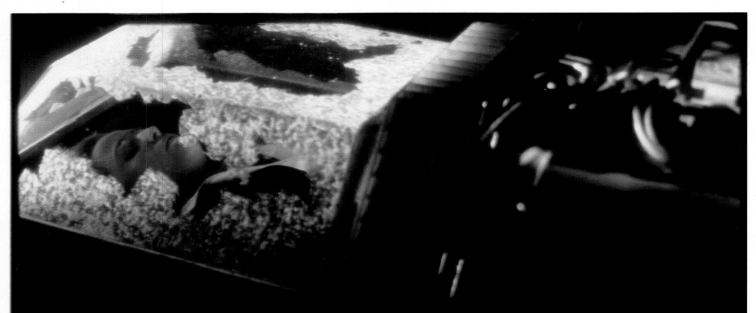

frame. Once on that set, Rob Bowman had quickly discovered that, no matter how he framed his shots, the camera wound up moving off the practical structure, requiring a digital set extension.

"It is a fact of filmmaking," Beck observed, "that you learn how to make a particular movie as you are making it. And when you're done making that movie, you could go back and make it again so easily. There's no question that there were times when Rob must have been frustrated on the interior spaceship set, feeling locked in as to where he could and could not move his camera. He'd ask: 'Can I move here? Can I move there?' And part of my job was to know when to say 'yes' and when to say 'no.' But Rob has such a good eye and such a passion

for the right shot, we were always stretching to give him what he wanted. He knows enough about effects to want to follow the rules and then, occasionally, break them. That's where the fun is, and the shots are often better for it."

Work on the set extensions at Light Matters began near the end of October. Shot by shot, Beck and his team determined if full 3-D computer modeling was necessary, or if a simpler, less time-consuming and less expensive 2-D approach would suffice. "I was always looking for places where we could use a 2-D solution," said Beck. "Most of the shots had to be 3-D because of the camera positions and movements. Whenever the camera was moving or dollying any distance, we had to

TUESDAY, OCTOBER 28: PLAYA VISTA

What was once the bustling Hughes Aircraft facility is now a string of abandoned office buildings and terminals. But the site's wide-open spaces and huge empty hangars are well suited to the filming of large-scale models for film production, and the crews for films such as *Batman Forever, Independence Day,* and *Titanic* have made good use of the facility.

Today, visual effects crews from Hunter/Gratzner Industries, Blue Sky/VIFX, and Light Matters are at the site, filming a twenty-three-foot building model for shots that will be incorporated into the live-action explosion, captured at the UNOCAL building four months ago. The wedge-shaped model is mounted on a four-foot-tall platform, and is surrounded by blue screens on all sides so that live-action elements can be matted into the model photography. Two large cranes stand nearby: one equipped with a camera, the other used by crew members to redress the top of the model.

Yesterday and the better part of the morning today have been spent shooting long shots of the building and a down-angle from the roof. For the down-angle shot, a rising ball of smoke and fire was ignited at the bottom floors of the model by miniature pyrotechnician Ian O'Connor. Simultaneously, monofilament wire attached to the exposed upper floors were released electronically, causing the floors to collapse, releasing dust and debris.

At midday, the crew sets up for a motion control shot that will pan across the decimated building. The computerized precision of motion control—a system by which camera moves can be repeated exactly—is required, since the pan will be composited with a live-action motion control shot executed on David Duchovny on location. A green screen card was placed in front of the actor for the shot, so that this model element could be inserted into the green matte area.

The model has been readied and the motion control camera is in place; but Mat Beck—who, with Blue Sky/VIFX visual effects supervisor John Wash, is orchestrating the model shoot—waits for the wind to die down before calling "action." "This wind is killing us," Beck says, under his breath. The wind is violently kicking up the dust and debris dumped from the top of the model, and flapping its small-scale government flags. Such activity will reveal the true scale of the model—filmed at ninety-six frames per second to create a sense of size and mass—when the high-speed photography is played back at normal speed. "That's going to look like it's in the middle of a hurricane," Beck mutters.

The wind dies down long enough to attempt a take of the panning shot. On Beck's "action," flame bars hidden within the model are ignited, debris is released from dumpers on the roof, and the computer-controlled camera makes its perfect sweep of the building. When Beck reviews the take on a video monitor minutes later, he is not happy with the way the debris is falling from the rooftop dumpers. "The debris should be falling *down* the building, not shooting out," Beck says to model supervisor Ian Hunter, whose crew has loaded the dumpers and rigged them to release their load on cue.

After a few more unsuccessful takes, Beck has an idea. "Forget the dumpers," he says. "Let's just get two guys with brooms up on the roof, and let them gently sweep out the debris on cue." The designated broom pushers are briefed on the preferred sweeping technique—a gentle push, not a violent shove—and they take their positions on top of the model, twenty-seven feet in the air, without protective railings.

When Beck again calls "action," the camera pans, the sweepers sweep, and the debris falls perfectly down the face of the building. With all the sophisticated technology available to a visual effects crew, sometimes success comes down to two guys with brooms.

model the set extensions in 3-D, since that movement created perspective shifts that could be duplicated only with a three-dimensional model. When the camera was locked off or farther away, we could get by with a 2-D digital matte painting." Many of the shots fell in between the two categories, requiring what Beck termed "two-and-a-half-D." "The two-and-a-half-D shots were basically 2-D images put through some sort of digital manipulation. Edson Williams could add a slight stretching or multiplaning to suggest a perspective shift. It was a way of cheating 2-D images so that they looked like 3-D images. It saved time, and in some cases it was actually a better way to approach a shot."

A shot of Mulder emerging onto the balcony of the ship, with the expansive interior revealed below, was a total CG fabrication, except for a small set piece in the foreground, on which David Duchovny stood. Everything else in the shot was synthesized in postproduction. "The balcony is supposed to be a hundred-some feet above the corridors where Scully's cryopod is sitting," Kurt Williams explained. "So when Mulder comes out onto this balcony, he has a wide view of this huge spaceship interior." Spotting Scully in the cryopod below, Mulder attempts to climb down to her, eventually sliding down a massive tube. The tube slide was shot with Duchovny's stunt double in the middle of August. "It was a forty-foot-long tube, surrounded by green screen

so that we could put a CG texture map around it, to make it look like it was part of the interior spaceship set."

More effects were featured later in the scene, when Mulder breaks Scully free from the cryopod and injects her with the alien virus vaccine, causing a reaction in the sleeping ship. "When Mulder injects Scully with the antidote," Beck explained, "it is almost as if the ship senses it. The antidote travels into a tube that is feeding Scully, causing a disruption in the ship's systems. That point had to be made very clearly with a shot of the feeding tube, filled with clear liquid flowing in one direction, as well as a shot of the amber fluid of the antidote flowing in the opposite direction, backing up into the ship's circulatory system, making the tube shrivel up and the ship start to shake and come alive. Both the fluids and the shriveling tube were modeled and animated in CG."

The most ambitious effects sequence of the film is featured in the climax, when Mulder and Scully climb their way out of the spaceship interior, onto the ice field, then run to escape the spaceship as it rises from its subterranean bed and takes off into the sky. The sequence was assembled with footage shot on the exterior spaceship set on stage, location footage from the Pemberton Ice Cap, and visual effects shots of a glacier tabletop miniature and model spaceship.

Onstage footage included shots of Duchovny and Anderson running on ice and through

opposite: Scully, infected by the sting of a virus-carrying bee, is transported to an Antarctica-based station via a cryolitter. **above:** Jim Martin's renderings of the cryobubble.

geysers of steam rigged by the special effects crew. For wider shots of the ice blanket imploding, green screen footage of the actors was composited into the glacier tabletop miniature, built by Scott Schneider and his model department at Blue Sky/VIFX. "Before the spaceship actually rises," explained Beck, "it heats up the bottom of the ice, making it fall in these huge sheets. It is an implosion rather than an explosion, a kind of ever-expanding 'disk o' death' that threatens to engulf Mulder and Scully as they run."

To simulate the effect, the sixty-by-twenty-foot tabletop miniature was equipped with sections that could be pulled out in sequence, creating collapsible areas of fake ice, baking soda, salt, and stearic acid—materials mixed to simulate a powdery top layer of snow. "The miniature was laid out over three tables, and these sections were pulled out like spokes in a wheel. As these large sections were pulled out and back, the fake snow and ice fell in. We kept yelling, 'Faster, faster!' And this huge thing did it. Bob Spurlock, who is a terrific model-maker and engineer, came in to help design the model." Unable to outrun the expanding ring of imploding ice, Mulder and Scully disappear into the chasm, reappearing on the spacecraft as it ascends from beneath the glacier. To simulate the effect of the characters rolling off a section of the ship, the actors had been filmed on a rising green screen platform, and those elements were composited with the spaceship model photography.

Built and filmed separately by Blue Sky/VIFX were two spaceship models: a six-foot, 1/200th-scale miniature of the entire ship—employed for full views of the ship rising and blasting off—and a 1/8th-scale, twelve-foot section for closer shots of the ship rising beneath Mulder and Scully. "Tim Flattery did some wonderful concept sketches of the spaceship," noted Beck, "then we translated those in 3-D in the computer at Blue Sky/VIFX so that we could show different views and also provide plans to a very talented Scott Schneider in the model department. Alison Yerxa was terrific in providing the surface detail that we eventually transferred to the model, through a process of graphic half-tone etching. I don't think it has ever been done before. That etching on the ship was a graphic metaphor for the show, hinting at details that are almost, but not quite seen and are constantly shifting in shadows and light."

"Blue Sky/VIFX also built a miniature ice station that was shot separately and composited into the model photography to look as if it was falling into the ice hole," said Beck.

Expansive background images of the glacial landscape were composited with both stage and miniature photography. "We went to the glacier location and took stills from every angle. Then, in post, John Wash and his guys at Blue Sky/VIFX built an environment out of those stills and composited that into the green screen area we had on stage or on the model." Also captured at the real glacier were wide shots of stunt doubles running across the ice, which were combined with the tabletop glacier elements.

While the building explosion and the interiors and exteriors of the spaceship constituted the major effects sequences in the movie, smaller effects were scattered throughout the show. Blue Sky/VIFX, for example, created CG bees to supplement the real bees shot on the interior bee dome set. Other visual effects provided appropriate backgrounds or suggested the passage of time, such as the transition from the ice cave of 30,000 years ago to the modern-day scene. "The camera pans to the black ceiling of the cave after we see the worms attack the primitive," explained Beck. "Then we see Stevie fall through that same ceiling, through the black. We took a little bit of cave ceiling detail from the B side—which was Stevie falling through—and added it into the ceiling of the primitive cave to create a transition that looked seamless, even though it was made up of two different pieces of film."

Also featured in the Stevie sequence is a long crane move that rises high above the cave and surrounding neighborhood to reveal Stevie's friends running for help, with the Dallas skyline in the distant background. The passage of time is suggested as the running children dissolve away and the crane moves back down to the cave opening—now surrounded by fire trucks and emergency personnel. "That was a relatively difficult shot for us," recalled Beck, "because we had to match the A side of the crane move, which was shot in the morning, to the B side of the crane move, which was shot later that afternoon. It required a lot of difficult tracking because there was so much wind out there in California City that day, the crane was bouncing around all over the place. It wasn't a smooth crane move at all." Stock footage of Dallas was simply dropped into the background, along the tops of the California City houses, to provide the appropriate skyline.

A background was also composited into shots from the bluff in Santa Clarita to reveal the bee domes and cornfield filmed in Bakersfield. "That view from the bluff was built out of several pieces," said Beck, "including the live-action foreground, the cornfield background, and a model train that was added, moving through the landscape. I had shot some very dark exposures on the cornfield, which was too brightly lit for these backgrounds, and we played around with those to make the background as dark and murky as possible. We did a lot of digital painting, taking the darker areas of the plate and replacing the brighter areas with them. We also put in a little CG smoke, just to tie all of the separate elements together."

Though Beck and his visual effects crew were still completing their slate of over two hundred effects shots, Bowman delivered his first cut of the film just before Christmas 1997, when it was screened for studio brass and Chris Carter. "I'd seen little sequences edited together before," Carter said, "but I waited to see the whole thing put together on the big screen. I was astounded by the amount of beautiful work that Rob had done. Ward Russell had also done a beautiful job, creating all of these big-screen, high-quality shots. I could see that we had a very good movie, and I was nothing but encouraged by it. That opinion was seconded by the powers-that-be at the studio when they came to see it. They applauded at the end of the movie. They turned to us and congratulated us. There were a lot of happy faces in the room."

Even with the studio's enthusiastic reaction and his own confidence in the film, however, Carter recognized that there was a lot of work to be done in the following four months. "I saw places where we could tighten," Carter noted, "places where we needed to expand things, places that might require reshooting. Most of it was a matter of editing and tightening, going over the footage again and again to see if we'd missed anything. We wanted to make sure that every moment played as well as it could, that every scene played as well as it could, that we were putting the best of our work on screen."

In the meantime, excitement was mounting as the June release date of the feature version of *The X-Files* neared. It started with buzz in both the mainstream and industry press and grew with the full-size posters that began appearing in movie theater lobbies. The first poster, which read 'Fight,' appeared in late November; the second, which read 'Future,' in early February; and the third, with the complete tag line, 'Fight the Future' in early March. Three trailers were planned, the first to appear with *Alien Resurrection* at Thanksgiving, the second with *Lost in Space* and *Mercury Rising* in the spring, and the third with *Godzilla* a month before The *X-Files* movie premiered.

A total of eighteen days of reshoots, additional photography, and inserts were scheduled for the last week of February, the first week of March and the end of April 1998. Although Carter had always been resistant to producing episodes of *The X-Files* that did not heavily feature both Mulder and Scully, that proved to be the only solution to finding the time for the movie reshoots. "We incorporated an episode that Gillian wasn't in at all," explained David Duchovny, "and that I was in for just a couple of scenes. We hoped the TV audience wouldn't feel cheated. It was the only way to do this."

Among the scenes on the reshoot schedule was the one with Mulder and the Lone Gunmen in the hospital, after the former has received a gunshot wound to the head. While the scene had originally been filmed at a real hospital on location, the reshoot was staged on a set at Twentieth Century Fox. "We weren't perfectly happy with that scene to begin with," recalled Chris Carter. "But we also wanted to reshoot it because we had gone back and forth with the idea of adding a car chase to that part of the movie. It had been in the original script, but it had never been budgeted or scheduled. I was in a hat-in-hand situation, going to the studio and asking for this added scene. They liked the movie as it was; and, in the end, I didn't get the car chase. It would have been very pricey and very time-consuming, taking David out of work on the series for more days than we could afford."

The reshoot of the Mulder/Lone Gunmen hospital scene also served to clarify the story. "It was a question of believability," said Duchovny. "I get shot in the head—but then I'm up and about, chasing

APRIL 10, 1998: AN INTERVIEW WITH MARK SNOW

Mark Snow, the composer who has provided the music for The X-Files *for all five of its seasons, was three weeks into composing the score when he sat down for this interview. In only twenty-four days, he would be in the scoring stage at Fox, conducting an eighty-five piece orchestra and recording the film's music score.*

J.D.: Most people don't know what is involved in scoring a movie. Would you explain the process?

M.S.: First, I write the music on my electronic equipment, the synclazier, which is a digital sampling music system. Then Chris Carter, the other producers, and the director's all come to hear that and make their comments. After I've made their changes, I bring in an orchestrator who listens to the music over and over and transcribes it for the instruments. That is the score that goes to the copiest who copies the parts out for all the players. And then we have four days of recording with the big orchestra, starting on May 4. The week after that, all of this music is taken to a mixing studio where we combine it and make it sound perfect. Then we put it in the six-track surround format for movies, and that is that.

J.D.: Is the theme from the television show going to be the movie theme as well, or were you asked to write something entirely new?

M.S.: A version of that theme will open the movie, but it is different than the television version.

J.D.: What are the specific challenges of scoring a movie, as opposed to a television show?

M.S.: Just the fact that we have an orchestra makes a huge difference. The scope of the sound is bigger and you have much more sound coming out of the movie theater speakers than you have coming out of television speakers. So I don't have to worry about having too much low-end or high-end sound, because it will all fit the spectrum of the big sound speakers. On TV you can't get too low or too high—everything has to be written in the mid-range. But for the movie, I'm freed from all the limitations of television's tiny speakers.

J.D.: What did you want to do with this score, musically?

M.S.: When the *X-Files* television show started, the music was mostly atmospheric. It was ambient sound effect music, with very little melody and little harmonic progression. In the last couple of years, it has become more musical, more melodic, more thematic. For the movie, there will be a combination of the atmospheric sounds and big, powerful music. There will be some scenes, for example, that will feature the electronics alone, without the orchestra, just to provide those ambient sounds. But a lot of the big, exciting scenes will have the full orchestra, playing more traditional movie music.

J.D.: Is there a part of this process you are most excited about?

M.S.: It is going to be a big thrill for me to record this at the Fox music scoring stage, which has been renovated recently. It is the best scoring stage in the city now. Everyone usually hears this music on the electronic equipment at my studio. Having them hear it fleshed out with the orchestra on this scoring stage is going to be incredibly thrilling. Also, it is going to be wonderful to conduct such a big orchestra—and *anything* that gets me out of my little room is fun.

after the bad guys? In the reshoot, we clarified that the wound wasn't that bad. So the scene is a little different, but not completely different. I did lose one of my favorite lines, which was when they tell me about the head wound and I say, 'Perforation, but not penetration.' Now that line is just one of those lost jewels...."

Also on the reshoot schedule was a newly written scene within the ice station in Antarctica. The exterior of the ice station had been filmed on the Pemberton Ice Cap the first week of production. But in the months since, Carter and his team had realized that the film needed an interior scene to underline the connection between the station and the subterranean spacecraft. An entirely new set was designed by the art department and erected onstage by the construction crews.

A final cut of the film—complete with 220 effects shots and music score—was delivered only one year after Chris Carter and his team had initiated preparations for the production. Going from prep to polished final film in a single year was an astonishing feat that had required teamwork, dedication, and commitment from every member of the cast and crew.

It was also a learning experience, especially for the television veterans who had taken up the mantle of feature film production for the first time with the *X-Files* movie. "I learned, more than anything else, that a film of this scale requires a tremendous amount of detailed preparation up front," Dan Sackheim observed. "It is deceptive, because in television you do so much with so little. So you think, 'Well, if I can prep a forty-five-minute television show in seven days, I ought to be able to prep a two-hour feature in ten weeks. But that isn't the case, because it is a completely different animal. It is so much bigger, so much more complex, with so much more exacting detail, you can't get away with things on the big screen that you can on the small screen. That was the lesson we learned on this show. But I also recognize that our experience in television, having to make decisions on the fly and having to do more with less was also tremendously helpful to us in producing this movie. It allowed us to come up with creative solutions that we may not have arrived at if we'd only done feature films."

Back on the set, Duchovny laughed with the crew between setups for the reshoot and reviewed the just-filmed scene on the video monitor. These on-the-spot monitor viewings were all he had seen of the movie, as he has chosen not to attend any of the screenings. "I don't really like to do that," he explained. "And I don't really *need* to do it. I know the movie is good because I know the producers and the director who made it are good. I trust them."

The comment suggested that there should, perhaps, be a revision to one of the show's most enduring tag lines: *Trust no one—except Chris Carter, Rob Bowman, Dan Sackheim, and Frank Spotnitz.*